Managing Risk:

A Guide for Physicians and Practices

Release date: December 15, 2013
Expiration date: December 15, 2016
Estimated time to complete activity: 7.5 hours

Christopher R. Jarvis, MBA, CFP®

CME sponsored by The Academy for Continued Healthcare Learning

By Christopher R. Jarvis, M.B.A.

Tel: (888) 527-8476

THIS PUBLICATION IS DESIGNED TO PROVIDE ACCURATE AND AUTHORITATIVE INFORMATION IN REGARD TO THE SUBJECT MATTER COVERED. IT IS AVAILABLE TO BE SOLD IN BULK QUANTITIES TO NON-LEARNERS FOR THE SOLE PURPOSE OF REDISTRIBUTION BY LAW FIRMS, SERVICE PROVIDERS AND LARGE MEDICAL INSTITUTIONS WITH THE UNDERSTANDING THAT THE PUBLISHER IS NOT ENGAGED IN RENDERING LEGAL, ACCOUNTING, OR OTHER PROFESSIONAL SERVICES. IF LEGAL ADVICE OR OTHER EXPERT ASSISTANCE IS REQUIRED, THE SERVICE OF A COMPETENT PROFESSIONAL PERSON SHOULD BE SOUGHT.
—From a Declaration of Principles jointly adopted by a Committee of the American Bar Association and a Committee of Publishers.

ISBN: 978-1-940648-03-3
Manufactured in the United States of America.

Continuing Education Information

To receive credit for this CME activity, participants must read the learning objectives and faculty disclosure information, read the full monograph, then follow these steps:

1. Go to www.accessCME.org.
2. Click on "Get Certificate" in the top left corner.
3. Enter the Certificate Code 2761311
4. Complete the post-test, and achieve 80%.
5. Complete the evaluation, and your certificate will be immediately available to you.

You may print or save the certificate for your files. It will also be sent to you via email to the address provided in your profile on www.accessCME.org.

Accreditation

This activity has been planned and implemented in accordance with the Essential Areas and policies of the Accreditation Council for Continuing Medical Education through the joint sponsorship of the Academy for Continued Healthcare Learning (ACHL) and Jade Risk. ACHL is accredited by the ACCME to provide continuing medical education for physicians.

Credit Designation

The Academy for Continued Healthcare Learning designates this enduring material for a maximum of 7.5 *AMA PRA Category 1 Credits*™. Physicians should claim only the credit commensurate with the extent of their participation in the activity.

Target Audience

This educational activity is appropriate for physicians practicing in the United States who are interested in reducing their risk for liability claims.

Statement of Need

It is critical for physicians to provide improved patient care by fostering better communication skills with patients and staff thereby reducing the risk of patient errors that may result in liability claims. The current practice of physicians as it relates to communication with patients and practice management specific to maintain low risk for liability claims has proven to be increasing areas of challenge for medical professionals. These areas are critical to continued patient care and with improvements and implementation of appropriate management systems can mitigate risk concerns on the part of the physician if implemented appropriately. Improving risk management strategies and enhancing patient communications will result in effective information exchange between the medical team and patients.

Educational Objectives

Upon completion of this activity, participants will be able to:

- Identify the principal risk factors that put physicians practices at risk for liability claims
- Identify the most common causes of malpractice/liability claims for the practicing physician, and apply defensive strategies
- Apply strategies to avoid and/or minimize risks of liability
- Discuss legal issues relevant to liability concerns in a variety of practice structures
- Use the assessment tools contained in this monograph to identify areas of risk, and formulate a strategy for corrective action
- Apply practice management strategies to provide improved patient care
- Apply communication strategies to provide improved patient care

Disclosure

Mr. Christopher Jarvis has disclosed that he has no relevant financial relationships with any commercial interest whose products or services are discussed in this material.

ACHL staff members and others involved with the planning, development, and review of the content for this activity have no relevant affiliations or financial relationships to disclose.

Disclaimer

All materials are included with permission. The opinions expressed are those of the faculty and are not to be construed as those of ACHL. For questions about the accreditation of this activity, please contact ACHL at 773-714-0705 x228 or mdaiga@achlcme.org.

ACHL policy on privacy: www.accesscme.org/terms

Note to Learners

This educational activity is available in two formats: PDF and e-book. Credit will only be awarded for participation in one of the two available formats.

Hardware/Software Requirements:

PDF:

- MS Internet Explorer 8.0 or higher, Firefox, Opera, Safari, etc.
- Adobe Reader 5.0 or higher

e-book:

- MS Internet Explorer 8.0 or higher, Firefox, Opera, Safari, etc.

About the Author

Christopher R. Jarvis, MBA, CFP®

Mr. Jarvis has an honor's degree in applied mathematics from the University of Rhode Island and an MBA from UCLA. As an actuary for Fortune 500 firms, he specialized in risk analysis and risk management. His firm, Jade Risk, LLC (www.jaderisk.com) assists physicians with risk management, practice structuring, and captive insurance arrangements.

As a lecturer, Mr. Jarvis has addressed the International College of Surgeons, American Medical Women's Association, Society of Gynecologic Oncologists, American Association of Neurological Surgeons and over 50 other medical groups and hospitals nationwide.

Mr. Jarvis is a co-founder of the Daktori Financial Fellowship program for doctors. More information can be found at www.Daktori.com or by emailing him at Jarvis@Daktori.com.

Acknowledgments

The authors would like to thank Dr. Lawrence Anderson and Dr. Svetislava Vukelja for their contributions to this work and for their efforts in reviewing the material.

Table of Contents

Introduction

Can We Do the Right Thing?

As a physician, it is no longer so simple to follow the adage "do the right thing" as it was in the past. When a physician began a general medical practice in the 1930s, the "right thing" meant taking care of the patient with the limited tools at hand, compassion and skill. While doing so, there was the absolute assurance from patients and society that the doctor was in charge.

For a physician of this era (as was the case for our fathers and grandfathers), the family home often doubled as the medical office. A pantry could be the examining room, a dining room the office, and an open front hall and parlor the waiting room. Office hours could be afternoons and evenings, with house calls and hospital visits in between. Moreover, there would be little, if any, office overhead; no receptionists, nurses, clerks or even billing services. In those times, the doctor was truly a "one person show" (and, almost exclusively at that time, a "one man show").

The pharmacologic armamentarium of the time consisted of aspirin, phenobarbital, sulfur, zinc and boric acid ointments, digitalis, mercury compounds, and a few others. The major tools battling disease were hope, faith, and the doctor's will. To the generation of the 1930s, 1940s, and early 1950s, the phrase "the will to live" was more than a slogan. Rather, it was a recurring reality in the battle with infectious disease. And it was the physician who was up front in that battle, holding high the flag of hope and knowledge.

We know that, for most of you, this is the image you still hold of yourself and most of your colleagues. And you should. Medicine is still a noble calling, and the best of us give of ourselves to our patients as we continue the fight against disease.

Why then is this monograph necessary? Why, if we are trying to do our best for our patients, are we attacked for the relatively few serious mistakes we do make? The answers to these questions are complex and will be examined in some detail later. Yet, behind these questions is the implicit assumption that we are on the right side of the battle. We are fighting the forces of disease and debilitation. We are trying to make people feel better and have more active and pain-free lives. However, physicians are no longer the only ones involved in this noble fight.

Today, the federal government, state governments, managed-care organizations and insurers want to be seen as leading the fight against disease. Hospitals, large group clinics, and even medical school clinical faculties may want to seize the battle flag from us. Consumer groups also want to lead our populace to "healthy living." Is it any surprise that the individual patients are unclear as to which flag to follow? Is it any surprise that some of us no longer seem to know which flag is leading in the right direction?

As confusing as this fight has become, we must remember that disease and ill health are still the enemy, not the other flag-bearers. Our obligation is first and foremost to our patients to improve their lives. The insurers, public policy groups, and health-maintenance organizations (HMOs), cannot, and should not, distract us from this primary responsibility.

It is often easy to become distracted from our priorities when we are besieged by the countless nuisances that sidetrack us in daily practice. Most prevalent of these are the pervasive government regulations (we discuss one such area in the chapters on HIPAA), as well as the underlying threat of malpractice and other liability risks. Whether they come in the form of an increase in the number of insurance forms, the practice of defensive medicine, or other symptoms, our attention is constantly from the main purpose of our professional goals: serving patients.

Written jointly by a practicing radiologist with more than 30 years experience, an asset-protection and risk-management attorney, and a former actuary, this monograph will address the principal threats that put your practice at risk for lawsuits: malpractice and others. Further, we will suggest ways to strengthen and protect you, so that you can securely and confidently keep your purpose—improved patient care— in sharp focus.

Once you understand the dangers that surround you, and learn effective strategies for avoiding and minimizing them, you will be better able to provide improved patient care. In this way, you will be able to more effectively "do the right thing" for each of your patients.

Chapter One

The Medical Malpractice Landscape in 2013

In the three years that have elapsed since the previous edition of this book, the medical malpractice landscape has changed a bit for the better, with a long way to go. Diagnosis-based claims continue to grow in their prevalence. Attempts to impose state government controls on malpractice lawsuits had some limited success, although the federal initiatives have stalled. Malpractice premiums have been falling slightly since 2005, but are still well above levels of a decade ago. The effects of the early part of the decade, where the cost of malpractice insurance forced physicians to move or curtail their practice areas, is still being felt.

Diagnosis-Based Claims Increasing

The trend toward malpractice claims for "failure to diagnose" has continued to rise during this time. Now accounting directly for over 50% of all malpractice suits, the charges of "failure to diagnose," "delay in diagnosis," or "improper diagnosis" are ones that affect a very broad spectrum of physician practices. While most of the largest multi-million dollar verdicts are still in the area of birth trauma and complications of surgery, many large verdicts are still of the "failure to diagnose" variety.

Obviously, the diagnostic area of malpractice liability has been gaining ground. In 2000, the median malpractice lawsuit verdict topped $1 million[1]—led by the category of failure, delay, or improper diagnosis of breast cancer and complications of pregnancy.

The number of successfully-litigated medical malpractice suits has been increasing slowly, but the number of multi-million dollar verdicts has seen a sharp increase in recent years. This has been particularly true in large cities, where inner city juries have awarded tens of millions of dollars in individual claims.

Medical malpractice cases settle—often for undisclosed amounts well into the millions of dollars. These cases take five years on average to "settle," and, during that time, attorney's fees have continued to climb. In fact, these fees have climbed well in excess of the increase in patient payments. Not only are plaintiffs' attorneys benefiting from protracted litigation, but defense attorneys for you and your insurance company have also seen a significant increase in their fees for each case as well. Insurance companies traditionally have delayed payments in any type of claim for as long as possible, so they could continue to collect premiums and earn interest on their money. So they too have been part of the long delay in case settlement. It appears, however, that these companies' out-of-pocket costs may be increasing faster than their earnings and they too are now complaining. The insurance companies finally may be on the side of the physician in wanting faster resolution of these cases.

The net result of such posturing and delay by all parties is that the average net income to both plaintiffs' attorneys has increased dramatically over the past five years. So the concern for physicians is no longer the percentage of successful cases against doctors or the rising average award size. The troubling reality is that it is now more profitable for attorneys to sue regardless of the merits of their malpractice case!

Consider the current income scenario. Lawyers "win" by achieving settlements in 1 of 3 cases they present, with an average payout by the insurance company of $335,000. If they collect on average 35- 40% of these payouts as professional fees, then each case they settle is worth $100–$130,000. Given this, is there any incentive for a lawyer not to file a malpractice suit? The claims would have to be so frivolous that the case would be thrown out at the earliest stage—summary judgment, perhaps. Unfortunately, very few cases are so extreme as to merit such an early dismissal.

Caps on Non-Economic Damages

One of the leading debates and areas of legislation in the last decade concerns the implementation of caps on non-economic damages in medical malpractice cases. In these types of cases, "non-economic damages" essentially mean payments for "pain and suffering." Determining the amount of non-economic damages is traditionally subject to broad discretion by juries, which try to equate pain and suffering to money— which is virtually impossible to do fairly and consistently.

Advocates of caps on such damages have argued that, without them, jury awards are inconsistent and unpredictable—forcing insurers to counter this uncertainty by charging higher premiums. Further, they argue that such unpredictability creates a major obstacle to out-of-court settlements, thus increasing litigation and the overall legal costs in the system.

Opponents to such caps argue that they penalize the plaintiffs who will endure the most pain and suffering are automatically punished. "By forever freezing compensation at today's levels, caps discriminate against a single class of Americans whose members are destined to suffer a lifetime of deprivation of dignity and independence."[2]

As of this writing, about half of the states have enacted some cap on either non-economic damages or total damages (only a few "total cap" states). A new trend that may work to reduce jury trials is a cap on attorney fees, regardless of the payout to plaintiffs. Florida is one state where this has been implemented. There is not enough data yet to judge its effectiveness.

Do Caps Work?

There seems to be some long-term evidence to support the claim that non-economic damage caps work to limit the growth of medical malpractice premiums. The best such evidence comes from California, the first state to implement non-economic damages caps in medical malpractice cases. In response to an earlier crisis in the early 1970s, California passed the Medical Injury Compensation Reform Act of 1975 (MICRA), which is often cited as a model for state legislation on such caps. Research has shown that between 1975 and 2000, malpractice premiums grew more slowly in California than they did in the rest of the Nation (167 percent vs. 505 percent).[3] Critics of this claim argue that the slow growth of insurance premiums may have more to do with the California insurance regulators than any impact the caps have had on damage awards, citing today's routine multi-million jury awards in California malpractice cases.

More recent data from the American Medical Association has shown that there may be some marginal effect in keeping physicians in a state, or attracting them to a state, when that state enacts cap legislation. According to a 2005 study published in the Journal of the American Medical Association (JAMA), the adoption of direct medical malpractice reforms that limit the size of awards led to a greater growth in the overall supply of physicians. Three years after adoption of reforms, the study found that the physician supply increased by 3.3 percent. According to the study, the direct reforms had a larger effect on: (1) The supply of non-group vs. group physicians; (2) The supply of most specialties with high malpractice insurance premiums; and (3) States with high levels of managed care.[4]

Conclusion

The malpractice crisis at the time of press continues to improve in terms of direct physician expenses. What has not improved, however, is the practice of defensive medicine. Finally national studies have begun to recognize and quantify this practice. Unlike the direct cost of malpractice insurance, which can be shown to be only a very small percent of medical costs, the practice of defensive medicine is felt to be very significant, with estimates of yearly cost from $100–178 billion.[5] State governments have taken significant action, most commonly in the form of enacting caps on non-economic damages in medical malpractice cases. The jury is still out, however, on what the long-term impact this will have on liability insurance premiums and jury awards. Even less clear is how this will help curb the practice of defensive medicine and the potential shortages we may suffer in attracting quality people to become physicians in high liability specialties.

We hope, in some small way, that this monograph will help you, the physician, not only practically—to reduce the risk of a medical error or liability event—but also psychologically—to help ease the stress that the present crisis may create for you in your own practice.

Chapter Two

Providing Care in Today's Malpractice Environment: A Land of Diagnosis-Based Claims

The malpractice landscape in the United States today is slightly improved over the past decade. Fewer malpractice claims are being paid[6] each year; but the average payment per lawsuit has been increasing. In 2008, the median malpractice claim paid was close to $200,000, a 10 year increase on the median from 1998 of over $50,000 (from $147,000 in 1998).[7] The average claim paid in 2008 (skewed because of a few very large cases) was $345,000—representing an 11% increase over 5 years since 2003.[8]

Perhaps even more significant than these statistics has been the shift from lawsuits arising in the hospital arena to those originating from outpatient situations. Not only have a wider cross-section of physicians been involved, but, increasingly, the burden for payment has been transferred to the individual physician rather than the hospital. A nationwide survey by a major insurer conducted in 1994 revealed that one of every seven physicians was involved in a malpractice suit. The PIAA 2009 study suggests an increase to one in 5.

In this chapter, we examine the changing malpractice landscape in depth. Specifically, we discuss how medical treatment has shifted to an outpatient scenario, how malpractice claims increasingly involve diagnosis-based claims, and how a fast-service mentality has put more time pressure on the practicing physician. Finally, we suggest ways to alleviate the time pressure in practice, which should lead to improved patient care and reduced malpractice risks by providing you with more time to diagnose, discuss, and document.

The Shift to Outpatient Treatment

Over the past 15 years there has been a continued shift toward outpatient medicine.

There are many reasons for this shift, but most can be separated into what we call either "push" or "pull" factors. Push factors are those pushing patients out of the traditional hospital setting, and pull factors are those pulling patients into outpatient clinics or offices.

Push Factors

The push to move patients out of the hospital and into the clinic or private office environment began with the advent of capitated payments to the hospitals in the form of Medicare diagnostic-related groups (DRGs). This early form of capitation initiated single global payments to hospitals for a single admission. Therefore, the faster patients were seen in hospitals, and the less that was done to them, the larger the potential hospital profit.

Although some hospitals still struggle with this philosophy, most have adapted to this shift. There has been a substantial decrease in hospital days per patient admission under these rules. With the advent of managed care, the pressure to decrease length of stay has been even more intense and the rise of for-profit hospitals has also furthered this trend. In some states, the pressure for early discharge has increased to the point at which the public and elected officials have become alarmed. State-mandated minimum length- of-stay for such procedures as normal birth and delivery and mastectomy have been instituted. The public, not the hospitals, have demanded this. This is a trend that we expect will continue.

Only recently has the impact of this push to shortened hospital stays been felt in the area of patient litigation. Patients and their families often resent this push outward to home or nursing facilities. For the physician, this resentment may result in a lawsuit, particularly if the patient, in retrospect, had been sent home too early. Complications of early discharge, particularly in the elderly, often propel patients to the physician's office or to the emergency department: sometimes, only hours after discharge. The physician is then in the position of having to either fight for readmission or manage the patient outside of the hospital. The potential for a liability suit in these circumstances is particularly high.

As managed-care organizations and hospitals increasingly dictate length of stay, the physician will assume an increasing risk for every hospitalized patient. Hospitals, many of which have up to 80% to 90% percent essentially capitated payments, are anxious to discharge patients earlier rather than later. Risk managers in hospitals too often look at the hospital's financial risk of longer stays rather than the physician's risk of assuming care for a too-sick patient outside the facility. In many states, outpatient malpractice claims have doubled since 1990, and it is likely this will continue as managed care grows. When we discuss managed-care liability issues, you will see how this "push outward" results in a higher exposure for the physician.

At the same time that hospitals and insurers are "pushing patients out of hospitals," there are aggressive groups "pulling patients into outpatient care." Those doing the "pulling" often have stronger motive to attract patients than traditional nonprofit hospitals have had.

Pull Factors

The "pull" for patients today often comes from the for-profit sector: frequently from large well-financed organizations. Fifteen to twenty years ago, outpatient surgical centers pioneered this revolution. Often, these were started by local physicians who saw an opportunity to lower costs for their patients, secure more convenient operating-room schedule for themselves, and make a small profit at the same time.

Gradually, these small, independent "surgicenters" were purchased by national companies seeking to establish a niche in the medical economy. The ability of these companies to pull patients out of hospital operating rooms with physician incentives became significant. Although these independent companies operated with little outpatient competition for a period, hospitals eventually realized that they could "compete against themselves" by setting up a for-profit division to handle the outpatient surgery. Hospitals frequently became part of a bigger corporation that had both for-profit and nonprofit arms.

Initially, only low-risk procedures were performed in these outpatient surgery centers. Over the past 10 years, however, more and more major procedures have been moved out to these locations. Although this move does not always correlate with increased outpatient liability, it is a major contributing factor. In one study, treatment-related and surgery- related claims constituted 43% of all outpatient claims.[9] OB/GYN and general surgery are most often involved. The percentage of litigation attributable to procedures in surgery has been decreasing in the 1990s. Although the reasons for this are not definitely proved, we have some observations that may be helpful.

The Shift to Diagnosis-Related Claims

Like the infectious organism that constantly changes and adapts to antibiotics and other drugs, the law of malpractice liability has been changing over the past 30 years. As malpractice defense lawyers constructed solid defenses to certain types of claims (particularly, failure to receive informed consent), plaintiffs' lawyers created new claims and found new sources of liability (most prevalent: diagnostic liability).

Over the past decade, partly as a consequence of increasing outpatient surgery, physicians and hospitals have focused their risk management on protecting against claims of failure to receive informed consent. Legal counsel eventually showed both doctors and hospitals how to successfully defend against these claims by telling the patient what surgery procedure he or she is going to have; what the benefit, complications, alternatives, and risks are; and documenting these conversations. Through the procedures and forms now accepted as standard practice, the physician transfers much of the malpractice risk to patients and their families. As long as the patient and family are competent to understand the conversation and the consent form, witnesses, and documentation are solid, a physician's defense barrier will be difficult to overcome despite an unfavorable result.

In this way, much of medical risk management in the 1980s focused on the informed consent issue, tightening up the forms, increasing the documentation, and requiring relatives to be present to sign. But lawyers are flexible, as is the law. If they could not overcome tight consent forms, they could look for theories of liability for which consent was not a key issue. Their most popular theory of liability is failure to diagnose.

Consent, in failure-to-diagnose cases, is almost irrelevant. Who would consent to one's physician failing to find out what is wrong with him? What would a defensive consent form look like? Perhaps something like this:

> *"As your doctor, I will use my best efforts to discover what is wrong with you. I do not know what tests I will order or what they will show. I do not know whether or not I will find the cause of what is bothering you or just a lot of other things wrong with your chemistry or anatomy that do not bother you. I do not know if what I will find will be significant in the long or short run.*
>
> *If I do find something to treat, I will try to find the medicine that will not make you sick or give you a worse reaction than the problem that you came in with. I will give you only such medicine as your insurer will allow. And if I can not order the right test or refer you to a specialist because of your insurer's restrictions, I will try to handle your problem as best I can.*
>
> *But because I am doing my best, you agree to all the above conditions and agree not to sue me, my office, and employees, even if we mess up."*

Obviously, patients would not sign this form.

Until this point, physicians' defense attorneys have not been able to design a solid defense to diagnosis- based claims by using a standard informed consent form. However, some state legislatures have begun to protect physicians by instituting preapproved standards of practice. If physicians follow these guidelines, they may bad physicians follow these guidelines, they may have an effective defense when bad outcomes occur. These statutes have not yet been tested extensively through cases, so it is too early to tell whether this defensive positioning will be successful.

Although an effective defense to diagnosis-based claims has not yet emerged, the number of claims continues to rise. Part of the reason behind this increase is that patients are being encouraged by the media to assign more liability to their doctors for diagnosis. Recent articles have advised patients to have the doctor document to them in writing the reason that a particular test is not necessary. Whether you think it is not necessary or the HMO thinks it is not necessary or too expensive, you put yourself in a tenuous legal position by signing such a document.

The end to this shifting pattern of litigation is not in sight. As long as it makes financial sense to do so, attorneys will continue to file lawsuits against physicians, especially those practicing in the most vulnerable areas. For the moment, it appears that diagnostic- related claims will be the main vehicle for liability. Within the broad heading of diagnosis-based claims are three theories of liability: (1) failure to diagnose; (2) delay in diagnosis; and (3) misdiagnosis. Each of these lends itself to litigation in many areas, but some general comments may help to further analyze the risk.

The entire spectrum of diagnostic-related claims seems to be a temporal one, with the three types of claims listed above as part of one continuum. Consider the following case study, which illustrates how these claims are interrelated.

Case Study

When first seen by a physician at the ER, an elderly woman presents, complaining of a fall outside her apartment. The emergency room physician who examines her quickly may diagnose her as having a hip fracture or bruise.

Here, if no x-ray films are ordered, the result may be a misdiagnosis of a soft-tissue injury alone. Alternatively, it may simply be an early case of delay of diagnosis if the fracture becomes clinically apparent 1 week later. It may even become a failure to diagnose if the occult fracture leads to a severe arthritis requiring a hip prosthesis months to years later. The basic facts for the patient's visit are the same.

Recommendation: From your common knowledge, conversations with colleagues, and professional periodicals, make a list of common misdiagnoses in your specialty/practice. Do the same for failures to diagnose and delays in diagnosis. By preparing and analyzing this list, you will better understand your vulnerability to the risks of diagnosis-based claims. Simply by becoming more aware of these liability sources, you are likely to put an increased importance on diagnosis and be less likely to rush to diagnosis.

The Pressure to Diagnose Quickly

To accurately understand today's malpractice liability environment, one must also consider how the time continuum is working against physicians today. Increasingly, the public has become accustomed to what we will call the "McDonald's mentality of service:" an expectation of standardized and very fast service. This mentality has slowly but steadily moved out of the traditional service industries and now has changed expectations of medical service for the outpatient setting or in-hospital stay. For the physician, this means that we are expected to heal our patients in less and less time: a time pressure that has made more difficult our ability to diagnose disease by observing its natural history.

The trend of pushing patients out of hospitals also allows for less diagnostic time and shorter intervals of clinical observation. Many hospitals require all diagnostic studies to be completed within 12 to 24 hours after being ordered, and many institutions strongly encourage testing to begin as soon as the patient is admitted. The critical pathways that hospitals create to streamline the work-up allows little time for "nature to take its course."

Since traditional medicine has used the progression of signs and symptoms to help diagnose disease, many physicians, particularly internists and general surgeons, have given up one of their most valuable tools in dealing with sick patients. Diagnostic testing is rapidly replacing diagnostic observation. Patients, hospitals, and insurers are all pushing physicians into quick diagnoses and quick diagnoses lead to a higher risk of misdiagnoses.

Unfortunately, the same pressures exist in the outpatient clinic or office setting. With office overhead rising, per-patient reimbursement falling, and new restrictions on testing and referrals, there is less time and less information with which to make accurate diagnoses. And this rapid spiral shows no sign of slowing. Again, misdiagnoses or failures to diagnose become increasingly common. Consider the following real-life case of an ordinary failure to diagnose. It demonstrates the danger of rushing to diagnose, which often prevents the physician from considering the most serious cause of symptoms. This oversight can have significant liability consequences.

The type of liability may not be revealed until the lawsuit is filed. Further, under many courts' rules, the plaintiff's attorneys need not choose any theory of liability when beginning the lawsuit, or even at trial. Thus, they might allege all three theories of liability and let the jury decide which one "fits the bill." As any observer of jury trials will confirm, juries may find for the plaintiff even when none of the claims are proved, only when certain elements of different claims are shown. This only makes a successful defense to diagnosis-based claim even more difficult.

Case Study

Mrs. Stern was a 50-year-old teacher in good health. On her first visit to the internist in May, she complained of some slight rectal bleeding but no other acute symptoms. The physician performed a quick rectal exam and found some internal hemorrhoids. He assured her that the bleeding was from the hemorrhoids, and sent her home on iron supplements.

The patient returned to the doctor's office in July. She still had rectal bleeding but her anemia was no worse. Her doctor looked quickly at her laboratory results, saw no change, and recommended she continue with the iron. As his schedule was extremely tight, the doctor moved on to the next patient. Over the next 3 months she experienced increasing fatigue. But when she spoke to the office nurse, she was told that the doctor was busy and that he would call her back. He never did.

When Mrs. Stern returned to the doctor in October, the physician realized that she was sicker than he had initially thought. He decided to admit her for further testing. A barium enema examination revealed a sigmoid mass. Surgery was uneventful, but the patient died 6 months later.

The case study of Mrs. Stern shows one subtle type of rush to diagnose. Rather than a blatant case study that involves a failure of the busy physician to listen to the patient initially, this case illustrates how even a good doctor, with a justifiable initial diagnosis, can be rushed into sticking to that diagnosis when further symptoms should lead him/her to investigate other possibilities. In this case, the malpractice was not the initial visit, but the follow-up visit, when the doctor failed to take the time to initiate a further workup.

Diagnosis-related claims may be different problems in different settings. In the busy office practice, delays may be compounded by the failure to get patients back to the office in a timely fashion or to notify them of the results promptly enough. Often this speed is out of the primary-care physician's control. Delays in getting results back from laboratories or specialists' reports mean delays in accurate diagnoses. This, in turn, means an increased risk of liability.

Recommendation: Give yourself more time by building strong telecommunications in your office. A top- notch telecommunications system can eliminate, or at least ameliorate, many of the potential hazards of this "rush to diagnose" age. Before specific recommendations are suggested, ask yourself whether you have adequate communications equipment to move data in and out of your office or whether the communication itself produces a delay in diagnosis. Any delay because of the telecommunications system increases the risk of liability to a diagnosis-based claim. Much time can be saved over a month or year simply by implementing an efficient, effective telecommunications system.

An efficient telecommunications system improves the quality of a practitioner's care not only because the physician and staff are less rushed, but also because the office is better able to meet patients' expectations for fast service. For example, the 45-year-old woman with a mammogram at noon on Friday might expect a report that afternoon. A weekend delay for her may be too long. A 2-week wait for a mammogram appointment may be reasonable for some but not for the woman who just found a lump in her breast. The greater the publicity surrounding the disease (such as breast cancer), the greater the pressure for rapid and accurate diagnosis. Patient satisfaction may be as tied to the timing of medical care as it is to the quality of that care.

Consider the following case study of a gynecologist, whose office recently instituted a modern telecommunications system in his office.

Case Study

Initially, some of his staff and patients complained about the new telecommunications system Dr. Dee established in his office. Now, all patients and staff members unanimously praise it. Staff members spend less time on menial activities (giving directions to the office asking the same questions of each patient), and patients are able to interact with the office efficiently, so they can get the information they want quicker.

For example, the voice-mail system has options for callers who want prescriptions refilled (they must have all pertinent information ready to record), need directions to the office, want billing questions answered, and even a hook to Dr. Dee's phone line. Of course, callers can always press "o" to speak to a staff member, and there is an emergency option prompt at the outset of the message. Also, the office is able to make good on its promise to respond to every message within 24 hours on workdays.

This case study briefly demonstrates one example of how a telecommunications system can improve patient care and free a physician and his staff from the incessant time pressures that exist today.

Depending on the structure of your practice and your area of practice, a telecommunication system may have different options. Consider the following recommendations in implementing a modern telecommunications strategy in your practice:

- Hire a communications consultant for your office. Perhaps your major insurers have such a program. If you are in primary care, the managed-care organization wants you and needs you. They have the resources to analyze and improve your practice management. And they should do this at their expense. If you can lower your practice overhead, you can provide care at lower costs and make you and the HMO more financially stable.

- Check with your hospital or the laboratories where your testing is done. They are the beneficiaries of your referrals. Have them install a fax machine in your office for your reports only. Consider buying a computer at the office with the capability to receive reports by e-mail.

- Consider a voice-message system. As the above case study demonstrated, such a system can free staff members to work on more meaningful duties and can improve patient satisfaction.

- Take a course on computer skills, particularly word processing and e-mail. Not only will you be leading your office by example, but your improved efficiency will reduce the business pressures on your time.

- Remember to consider the issue of patient confidentiality when information and report transfer options are concerned. Be sure that everything in your office is in a secure location, removed from the gaze of patients' prying eyes. If e-mail becomes the preferred mode of information transfer, make sure passwords are used to limit access to confidential information.

Chapter 2: Self-Assessment Checklist

The following are common signs that a physician may be susceptible to making a quick diagnosis. Use this checklist to evaluate your own behavior and as a preventative reminder to slow down and make more thorough analysis before diagnosing or staying with a diagnosis.

1. Do you spend a decreasing amount of time listening to patients, failing to obtain critical information?
2. Do you spend less time in a physical examination of patients and therefore miss key signs?
3. Do you rely too often on "playing the odds" for the most common diagnosis?
4. Do you rule out the worst or most severe diagnosis without proper justification rather than considering all the alternatives?
5. Do you order only the routine tests and fail to consider less usual possibilities?
6. Do you take only a new patient's history related to the specific complaints of the visit rather than his/her full medical history?
7. Do you take cursory notes in the patient's chart that might be difficult to read or interpret if your diagnosis is ever challenged after the fact?
8. Have you contacted your referral specialists to create a rapid and established method of receiving their reports?
9. Do you have a voice-message system at your office? For each physician?
10. Do you get your outside lab reports faxed, mailed, or e-mailed to you?
11. Do you dictate your notes or write them down? How long does it take for your staff to transcribe the dictated notes?
12. Have you considered voice-recognition software to transcribe notes?
13. Ask outside physicians who try to speak with you on the phone: "How long does it take to get me on the phone?" Perhaps you need additional phone lines.

14. Ask new patients who want to schedule an appointment: "How long does it take to get the staff member on the phone?" or existing patients who are awaiting reports: "How long does it take to get the staff member on the phone?" Perhaps a voice-message can route these calls more efficiently.

No matter what time pressures you are under, never fail to do the following:

- Thoroughly examine the patient.
- Take and document a thorough history.
- Conduct those diagnostic tests and procedures generally considered appropriate and those that rule out the most serious diagnoses.
- Carefully eliminate alternative modes of diagnosis and treatment.
- Set up an efficient communication system, particularly for patient follow-up.

Chapter Three

When Liability Can Begin: The Doctor-Patient Relationship

The establishment of a doctor-patient relationship and malpractice liability are intimately related. Unfortunately, the establishment of the doctor-patient relationship is much less formal than one would expect. Most of us are conditioned to believe that this relationship starts when the doctor sees the patient in a formal consultation or another in-office situation. The courts, however, have not always followed such a narrow definition. Under the law in this area, a written contract or other documentation between the parties is not a prerequisite to the doctor-patient relationship. In fact, the patient need not have ever visited the doctor's office, or even spoken with the doctor, for the relationship to begin and for a standard of care to be imposed.

In this chapter, we will examine the most common ways an informal doctor-patient relationship is established and how to avoid these liability-creating scenarios. We will also discuss a risky area of the relationship once it has been established: the physician's duty of confidentiality. Finally, we will provide case studies to demonstrate real-life situations in which clinicians are put at risk because of these issues.

Informal Social Setting

The first type of doctor relationship that we should consider is that which has been established in an informal social setting. One ordinarily does not think of casual advice given to an acquaintance or a friend as establishing the doctor-patient relationship. In most cases, this is not a problem. However, let us take the example of the acquaintance (named Al):

If Al can show that a doctor-patient relationship existed by your conversation, the law will measure your actions against a reasonable standard of care: what other physicians in your medical community would have done under similar circumstances.

As physician experts can always be found to say you did not do enough—that is, make the diagnosis that Al might have risked having a myocardial infarction, that Al should have gone to the emergency room, that Al should have called you later that day—you could easily be held liable in this situation.

Case Study

Al, a friend of one of your golfing friends, tells you about some mild back pain while you are both out on the golf course. You suggest that this is probably due to minor muscle strain and that Al should come see you in the office on Monday morning.

In the interim, however, Al becomes sicker, and his wife urges him to go to the emergency room. Having spoken with you, Al feels reassured and tells his wife that there is no need to do so. When conditions worsen, however, he ultimately winds up in the emergency room with an acute myocardial infarction, which has progressed to the point at which serious complications ensue. Although he had never sought formal consultation from you, Al may have relied upon your advice that this was only a mild muscle strain. Relying on your advice, a reasonable thing to do under the circumstances, Al chose not to visit the hospital earlier.

What can we learn from Al's case study? First, even the most innocuous conversations in informal settings can be interpreted by patients in ways that actually reduce the quality of the medical care given to them. Moreover, these seemingly innocent conversations can create liability. Further, as a potential target, the physician should always consider the liability ramifications of even casual advice. If you are going to give medical advice, you should expect to be held accountable for that advice, no matter how informal the situation and no matter how the patient acts on that advice.

Recommendation: Whenever possible, avoid giving medical advice in informal settings. Recommend that people see you in the office (or at home) before you make a diagnosis or advise any course of treatment. If informal advice is given, make sure that the patient is followed up promptly with an office or hospital visit.

Telephone Advice

In the chapters on miscommunication and on managed- care risks, we will analyze the dangers of telephone advice. Nonetheless, it is important to discuss here because it is often a means of creating the doctor-patient relationship. Perhaps even more common than the conversation with an acquaintance in a social setting is the situation in which a friend, colleague, or family member calls for medical advice. Many of these people are not, in fact, our patients before the phone conversation. This may not be true after the call. In short, the doctor-patient relationship can be established over the telephone.

The most dangerous element of creating a doctor- patient relationship by telephone is that you have deprived yourself of the opportunity to see the patient in person and to examine him. Therefore, it is much more likely that suggestions that you make will turn out to be erroneous. It is not uncommon in these situations to make a diagnosis or recommendation over the phone that you never would have done in person, had you had the opportunity for a physical examination.

Recommendation: Avoid giving medical advice to potential patients or potential patients over the phone; Recommend that they see you in the office (or at home) before you make a diagnosis or advise any course of treatment. If you must give a telephone consultation: Document, Document, Document! As you're not seeing the patient in person, you are relying on their description, not your own observation. Write "the patient says she has no back pain" rather than "there is no back pain."

Payment and Place Not Controlling

Unlike ordinary contracts, the existence of the doctor— patient relationship is not dependent upon "consideration" (charging of a fee). Money (or anything else of value) need not change hands for the relationship to be established. Whether or not the patient pays you, either through insurance or directly, is irrelevant to your relationship with him. All patients have the same rights to your services and to the same standard of care, regardless of payment.

It is not necessary to actually see or talk with the patient for the doctor-patient relationship to be established. If, for instance, you are on vacation and have hired a substitute to cover for you, you may be liable for the acts of your substitute. The law will imply the relationship between you and the patient through your substitute, who has become your agent for medical services.

Self-Assessment

How do you hire substitutes now? Is there any formal record-keeping for the hiring process?

Recommendations: When you agree to hire someone to replace you, make sure that the replacement has the same level of medical competence that you have. Document your search for a competent replacement and the qualifications process, if any. Keep copies of your correspondence with the substitute(s) and their resume(s) and curricula vitae.

Recognize that because the substitute is new to your patients, there may be more distrust and the doctor-patient relationship, and the medical treatment itself, may suffer as a result. It is important, therefore, that you instruct anyone covering for you on those areas that you consider to of high risk such as potential emergencies or referrals.

Patient Confidentiality

One aspect of the physician—patient relationship that can cause a great number of problems is patient confidentiality. You must be absolutely certain that, in the physical layout of your office, the patient's medical and financial information is not accessible to other patients. Doing a reasonable job to minimize disclosure of confidential information is not enough. You must prevent such disclosures absolutely or risk liability.

You also must be certain that, in the information transfer involved in billing, a patient's confidential information is not mistakenly disclosed to individuals or companies that have no legal right to obtain it. A written release form is necessary for you to give any of this information to a third party. Make sure you use it. Often, insurance companies and lawyers will attempt to gain confidential information through telephone calls to your staff. Unscrupulous collection agencies may even call your office asking for information on patients under the guise of medical insurance.

Recommendations: Train your staff to deflect all questions that relate to a patient's confidential financial or medical information. Instruct all staff that such information should never be made available without previous written authorization from the patient.

If you use an outside billing service, make sure that they follow the same guidelines. Just because they are not your direct employees does not mean that you will not be liable for their indiscretions.

Chapter 3: Self-Assessment Checklist

Assess your physical office set-up for patient confidentiality. Get out a diagram of your office or clinic premises and re-identify the individual points of patient interaction. If no such diagram exists, create one, using the following guidelines:

1. Where do new patients sit for initial data interviews? Does only one person collect the information? Is it visible to other office staff? What about to other patients? Do you have clear glass partitions? Would one-way glass be preferable? If you have older patients, is there room for an accompanying spouse or child to sit?

2. Are our areas of confidential information gathering soundproof? Sit outside the area yourself and have your staff role-play as patient and clerk. Can you hear their conversation? If you can, make sure you correct the problem.

3. Are patient exam rooms visually protected and soundproof? Can patients or staff see or hear you? Do not trust thin walls to block all conversations. An overheard conversation can embarrass patients and create liability if the patient's identity is revealed when he/she leaves the room.

4. Do you have the type of practice in which your patients do not want their names known to others under any circumstances (certain plastic surgery practices, clinics where sexually transmitted diseases are tested, etc.). If so, how do you call these patients into your office or examination room. Consider an impersonal or coded system upon check- in, so names or initials are not used. Even a local area beeper system for each patient may be cost effective and very private.

5. To test these issues in your practice, consider asking a close friend or colleague to pose as a patient in your office: spend time in your waiting room, examination room, corridors. They will be able to give you an unbiased view of your office and staff currently handling these concerns. Just be careful not to distress your staff during such a "test."

This space is provided for the purpose of creating a diagram of your office/ clinic space using the guidelines on the preceding pages.

Chapter Four

Managing Diagnosis-Related Liability: What We Can Learn From Closed Claims

Analysis of closed claims data provides one of our most reliable tools in predicting future malpractice risks. We can survey not only the types of cases accounting for the current malpractice epidemic, but we can also predict future trends. An in-depth analysis allows us to probe the reasons behind many lawsuits, to profile a typical plaintiff and defendant, and to analyze the type of situations that lead to litigation.

The Physician Insurers Association of America (PIAA) continues to provide a great service in this analysis. This association of dozens of national and local malpractice insurers provides detailed reports in specific areas. With combined coverage of more than 100,000 physicians, their statistics are large enough to be meaningful and they have developed excellent survey and reporting techniques. By using their recent studies as an example, we will see how this type of data can help us understand the risks involved in individual medical practices.

In this chapter, we will examine the results of three large PIAA studies: claims involving breast cancer and myocardial infarctions. In addition, studies of lung and colon cancer claims will be briefly analyzed. Here, we maintain our analysis of the same studies reviewed in the prior version of the monograph, as there have not been studies since that impact our conclusions materially.

Breast Cancer: Lessons From a PIAA Study

The PIAA breast cancer survey is useful to examine because, in a number of cases, this area now constitutes the largest single category of malpractice claims. The dollar total of these claims is second only to obstetric and delivery-related cases. Furthermore, many physicians have contact with patients with breast cancer, and many groups of physicians are involved in the lawsuit analysis. We also have the advantage of three surveys: one in 1990, one in 1995, and the latest in 2002.[10, 11, 12] These demonstrate changes in trends in the malpractice landscape.

The first and most obvious trend in malpractice related to breast cancer (as noted in earlier chapters) has been the shift from claims involving surgery or procedures to diagnosis-based claims. Whether the claim was failure in diagnosis, misdiagnosis, or delay in diagnosis, this category of claims continues to climb. We have already examined some of the reasons for this trend.

The important thing to acknowledge here is that the diagnostic claims can involve many, if not all, types of generalists and specialists: much more so than surgery- or procedure-oriented claims. In the mammography studies, the categories most often involved were radiologists and primary-care physicians. Gynecologists, surgeons, pathologists, and oncologists were also involved. In a limited number of cases, hospitals and larger entities were affected.

Liability Factors and Causes

Three major factors play a significant role in propelling the category of diagnostic claims regarding breast cancer to the forefront of liability. First, there has been tremendous publicity about breast cancer, particularly from women's groups and popular periodicals. Second, the disease is common. Almost one in eight women will have a diagnosis of breast cancer sometime in her lifetime. Third, the public has been told continuously about the importance of early diagnosis in saving lives. Add to these factors the simple fact that diagnosing breast cancer early is not easy, and one has a situation ripe for liability.

As physicians, we may have over-sold ourselves to the public, creating the impression that we can easily diagnose and cure breast cancer before we have developed the tools to accurately diagnose the disease consistently at an early stage. Given this scenario, it is easy to see why so many malpractice cases related to breast-cancer diagnosis have surfaced. If the public believes that we can find this disease and cure it easily, they will become angry when we do not. And with approximately 44,000 deaths annually, their anger is easily understood. If we are not going to admit our shortcomings in the ability to diagnose breast cancer early, we can expect the number of lawsuits to increase.

If every patient with the possibility of getting breast cancer were referred for annual mammographic screening, we might expect that the radiologist reading these mammograms would be the dominant lawsuit target. Yet, the most recent study showed that although radiologists were the number-one defendant group, they accounted for only 33% total of physicians named in lawsuits.[13] This was up dramatically from 11% 10 years earlier, reflecting the increasing trend toward mammography in the country.[14] But what of the other groups?

Family doctors and internists who had previously accounted for 26% of all physicians involved in lawsuits, dropped to the fifth position at 8% in 2002. Obstetricians and gynecologists remained at 23%, surgical specialists 14% and all others 12%. Interestingly, the third largest group were not physicians, but their corporations, accounting for 12% of all claims.[15]

The leading cause of lawsuits included a failure to refer the patient for a mammogram, a missed palpable lump on physical examination, a disregard for the patient's breast symptoms, or a dismissal of her request for a mammogram. Also significant were failures to properly diagnose mammography and a negative mammogram report with failure to follow- up with the patient. However, the largest category of lawsuit claims arose from the failure of the physician to be impressed by the physical examination or the patient complaints and the resultant delay in diagnosis or treatment.[16]

The above causes appear to be fairly straightforward failures of either knowledge or communication. We have to ask why this occurs. It may be because there is a widespread belief that breast cancer is asymptomatic until very late in its course and that, in younger premenopausal woman, the disease is relatively uncommon. Such beliefs appear to be widely held among all physician groups. In fact, reviewing these cases, we can see the growth of lawsuits reflecting our continuing education process in understanding this disease.

PIAA did a careful interview study of the women who had filed lawsuits.[17] They found that, indeed, many cancers were not asymptomatic. In fact, although a painless mass was recorded as the most common symptom in 46% of the cases, painful or tender breasts (with or without a mass) was the patient's reason for presentation. If, as the treating physician, you assume the pain is due to a cyst, you will be correct the majority of the time, especially for younger patients. However, a significant minority of the time (25%) you will be wrong. If so, you will face a tragic situation in terms of the patient's health and possibly significant legal liability. To provide better care for your patient and to avoid malpractice liability, follow these important recommendations.

Recommendations: When a patient presents with any complaints referable to the breast, even at a relatively young age, consider the worst possible diagnosis:

cancer. Unless you are absolutely familiar with the complete and actual history and symptoms of the disease, DO NOT EXCLUDE YOUR MOST SERIOUS DIAGNOSIS ON HISTORY ALONE. This could be a serious mistake.

The PIAA study noted above also demonstrates that breast cancer is not uncommon, even in young premenopausal women. Do not assume that, because you do not hear much about a common disease in a young or older age group, it does not occur. This attitude can be extremely dangerous. In this study, most of the lawsuits and most of the paid settlement amounts were to women under 50 years of age. In fact, the younger the woman, the higher the individual case settlement value.

Women in their 20s and 30s accounted for 40% of the total dollar liability, including all women in their 50s, 60s, 70s, and 80s.[18] The total years of life lost was greater for women in their 40s than for women in their 60s, when the disease is more prevalent. The lesson: The younger the patient, the greater the liability.

Do not dismiss diagnosis simply because the patient is in a "low-risk" age group. Consider the following case study as a reminder:

Case Study

Carol B was an active tennis player, aged 34 years. With some intermittent back pain, she visited her internist's office. Her symptoms were not severe and responded to analgesics and an exercise program. While at the doctor's office for her next 6-month visit, Ms. B mentioned to the doctor the slight, but definite, pulling pain she had been experiencing in the left breast. Physical examination revealed a lumpy breast, and the doctor told her he was sure it was cystic disease, which she had experienced before.

At her next appointment 6 months later, Ms. B again mentioned the breast pain. The physical exam had not changed. Ms. B had thought very little about the discomfort although it was present most of the time. Again, the doctor reassured her that he felt that this was cystic disease of the breast and she should not worry about it.

One morning, she thought she felt a new lump in that breast. She was due for her annual gynecologic examination 3 weeks later and pointed the lump out to the gynecologist at the visit. Despite what he felt was a normal physical examination, the gynecologist ordered a baseline mammogram. A finely calcified small mass was discovered measuring about 1.5 centimeters. The patient underwent excisional biopsy, laser lumpectomy and radiation. Despite what seemed to be adequate treatment, she died 2 years later. The estate successfully sued the internist, alleging delay in diagnosis leading to death.

Here, Ms. B's internist was in a difficult situation. Although he found a lumpy breast upon physical examination, because of Ms. B's young age, he did not feel it necessary to rule out breast cancer with any type of further study on the first visit. Statistically, this course of action seemed reasonable. However, when she again presented with symptoms of breast pain, the wisest course of action would have been to ignore the statistics (which would point against breast cancer) and rule out the most serious diagnosis leading from the patient's complaints. Here, that most serious diagnosis would have been breast cancer.

Risk Assessment and Screening Guidelines

An important question for the clinician to ask is "Can you trust national society recommendations when it comes to screening this common disease?" The American Cancer Society, which less than ten years ago opposed screening women under age fifty, now strongly recommends annual mammographic screening in the 40- to 50-year-old age group. But even years ago the statistics from the Physician Insurers Association of America have shown that 33% of all claims for missed breast cancer were from women under 40 years of age.[19] Our conclusion must be that if there is any clinical or statistical suspicion of breast cancer at any age, mammography and/or ultrasound should be ordered.

This choice would reduce the likelihood that you will miss a cancer diagnosis and/or be sued for failure to diagnose. However, this alternative may run you afoul of insurance company guidelines and financial incentives. Our duty is to act in the best interests of our patients, despite frustrations with insurance company officials and their guidelines.

Assessing risk profiles can be aided by studies such as those of the PIAA. According to their latest study, the average patient suing for breast-related diagnosis is a young (under 50) and often healthy woman. Unlike the plaintiffs of 15 years ago, who sued almost exclusively because of complications of treatment, today's patients frequently sue because of failed expectations in diagnosis or the inadequate physician response to their complaints.

Often, the disgruntled patient is most upset that the physician did not recognize the early symptoms that presaged the severity of the disease, no matter how innocuous the symptoms appeared at the time. This is especially dangerous for the clinician with cases in which minor symptoms could be caused by a host of both major and minor diseases. By relying too heavily on statistics and odds, you may fail to rule out the most serious pathology.

For example, everyday in emergency rooms physicians see the "mild mid-back pain patient" who returns two or three times. The most common diagnosis is that the patient is suffering from muscular skeletal pain. However, the patient may eventually demonstrate a dissecting aortic aneurysm. Such a missed diagnosis can lead to tremendous liability.

A slight right lower quadrant pain and low-grade fever in an older patient may increase in severity over a few days, turning out to be a ruptured appendix with peritonitis. There is no easy solution to the problem of diagnosis-related lawsuits.

To ensure the highest level of patient care and maximal avoidance of liability, you must follow our recommendation to always *consider and rule out the most serious diagnosis.*

Myocardial Infarctions: Lessons From a Leading Story

Failure to promptly diagnose and treat myocardial infarction is a common mishap in medical practice and is a frequent allegation in medical malpractice lawsuits. Thus, it is valuable to be able to analyze a closed claims study of this type of lawsuit.

The PIAA myocardial infarction study involved 349 paid cases, in which 495 physicians had payments made on their behalf.[20] In slightly more than half of the cases involving diagnosis-based claims, the patient presented in the provider's office, whereas in one third of these cases, the first contact with the patient was in the ER. In terms of specialties, family physicians were sued most frequently, with cardiologists surprisingly the fifth most common defendant group

This study pointed out the fallacy that risk analysis for myocardial infarctions should be calculated only by age and history. Although high incidence of risk factors was present among those who suffered myocardial infarctions (44% had hypertension, 43% smoked, and 22% suffered from hypercholesterolemia), almost 70% of the group had no previous history of coronary artery disease, and 83% had no previous myocardial infarction. Further, 47 percent of claimants were under the age of 50.

The overall average payment in myocardial infarction cases was around $300,000, but for the 30 to 39- year-old patient age group, it averaged $470,000, confirming that much of settlement amounts in these cases are replacement of lost wages, which are higher for younger patients. (These numbers are gleaned from cases that, overwhelmingly, are settled before any trial phase).

Perhaps the most revealing aspect of the PIAA study is the data on the diagnoses involved in the cases. Continuing with the trend we mentioned in Chapter 1, in this study, pure diagnosis-based claims (195) clearly outnumbered both therapeutic-based claims (45) and claims involving both diagnostic and therapeutic errors (109).

Although pain was the most common complaint of patients in the myocardial infarction study (83% of all patients reported pain as the initial symptom), what was most interesting was the physician's initial impressions of these cases. In 26% of the cases, the doctors diagnosed the pain to be of the gastrointestinal origin or (in 20.7% of cases) of muscle origin.

These initial impressions may help to explain why, in 65 of the cases, no diagnostic studies were ordered and, in 170, no electrocardiograms. Common tests performed were cardiac enzymes (60), chest radiographs (58), other laboratory tests (29), and stress tests (16). In essence, the physicians involved in these cases failed to consider the most serious diagnosis and rule it out by testing it.

Nonetheless, ordering the proper test is not the end of liability-risk factors. Still, it must be interpreted accurately. In the PIAA study, failure to properly interpret the test or failure to get the results promptly were a liability factor in 57% of cases in which an electrocardiogram was ordered. Lack of expertise and failure of communication continue to be problems.

The PIAA study on myocardial infarction stands as a powerful illustration that, in order to enhance patient care and limit liability, clinicians must maintain a high suspicion for coronary artery disease, regardless of whether the patient presents in-office or in an emergency room and even if the patient does not fit the typical high-risk profile.

Physician Group	***No. of Payments***
Family/General Practice	160
Internal Medicine	109
Emergency Medicine	75
Cardiology	34
Other Specialties	35
Surgical Specialty	9
Physician Extenders	4
Corporation	2
Hospital	57
Total	495

Recommendation: Do not be misled by "traditional" low risk factors such as youth, lack of a history of heart disease, or gender. Many members of these low-risk groups suffered myocardial infarctions and became claimants in this study. As we mentioned earlier, always consider the most serious diagnosis when patients present with symptoms that could possibly be related to myocardial infarction, then rule it out through testing.

Specific Recommendations From PIAA Myocardial Infarction Study

- Document all patient complaints relative to pain/ pressure and its location.
- Document any family history of heart disease and all personal history of heart disease including complete risk factor profiles.
- Request and document the results of any previous evaluative cardiac studies and compare the results of any present studies to the previous studies.
- Follow any patient presenting with any symptoms indicative of a heart condition until the diagnosis is ruled out, even if diagnostic testing is inconclusive and even if the patient is relatively young.
- If clinical suspicion is present, despite unchanged or negative electrocardiogram, recommend an exercise tolerance test.
- Have the same index of suspicion for the patient who presents in the office as for the one who presents in an emergency department.
- Promptly report any positive test findings to the referring physician, and follow up with other physician consultants regarding tests, etc.

Also, create a handout from the information in below, recommended by the PIAA, to your patients. This will educate patients about the seriousness of myocardial infarction and will improve communication between the patient and you, allowing you to make more accurate diagnoses.

Providers' Initial Impressions in Cases with Misdiagnosis

MI	2.6%
CAD	4.6%
Anxiety	5.3%
Respiratory DX	6.3%
Angina	6.9%
Other	13.2%
Cardiac Etiology	14.5%
Musculoskeletal	20.7%
Gastrointestinal	26.0%

Lung and Colon Cancer Studies

Three studies by PIAA—one in 1991 on colon cancer and two on lung cancer (1992 and 2004) — also demonstrate the increasing prevalence of diagnosis- based claims.[21, 22, 23] Further, these studies show that clinicians cannot simply rule out a cancer diagnosis simply by relying on the classic risk factors such as age and family history.

In all 3 studies, a failure or delay in diagnosis were significant reasons leading to claims. In the colon cancer study, failure to diagnose or delay in diagnosis were most often due to failure to refer for endoscopic or barium examination (79%). Failure to respond to the patient's complaint (19%) and failure to check for questionable bleeding (15%) were also significant factors. Failure to refer to a specialist was a factor in 15% of the cases.[24]

In the original 1992 lung cancer study, delay in diagnosis was due to inadequate evaluation (60%) and/ or failure to respond to an abnormal x-ray film report (44%). Failure to communicate was claimed in 20% of the cases.[25]

In the most recent study of 2004, however, these numbers had reversed. Inadequate evaluation dropped to 20% of causes, but failure to communicate results to the patient satisfactorily rose to 50%![26] In all studies, a lack of advanced age as a risk factor did not prevent mishaps in patient care and resultant malpractice claims. In all studies, in fact, close to 30% of claimants were under 50 years of age. Further, as in the above studies, indemnity payments were generally higher in the younger groups. Specialties most often named in the studies' claims included family physicians, internists, radiologists, and general surgeons. Surprisingly, in the 1991 colon study, gastroenterologists were named in less than 5% of cases.[27]

Lessons

What, if anything, can we learn from all of these studies as a whole? First, we would urge you to obtain your own copies of these studies, available at $20 each from the PIAA. Beyond this, we see some common lessons from which every clinician can benefit.

The worst or most serious diagnosis is the one you do not want to overlook. Even if you consider the serious problem unlikely, you should put it under the "rule-out" category and document all other negative supporting data. In both the breast cancer and myocardial infarction studies, failure to diagnose because of a patient's young age or atypical symptoms lead to poor outcomes and physician liability. The old adage "plan for the worst, hope for the best" is very true in diagnosis liability.

Diagnostic related claims are not going to decrease. They represent the leading theory of liability for clinicians in almost all specialties. Be prepared. If there are approved practice guidelines in your area, follow them. If your patient population is high risk because of age, social, or economic factors, calculate that into your planning. This is one area in which a good defense is critical.

As a patient, you can assist your doctors in making a timely diagnosis and providing the correct treatment.

- Take the possibility of a heart attack seriously, even if you first see your doctor in his or her office.
- Discuss any family or personal history of heart disease.
- Mention any pain and pressure and its location.
- Cooperate with your doctor to continue pursuing a complete diagnosis if you have symptoms that could indicate a heart attack such as pain or pressure in the chest area and shortness of breath. Do not assume it is just a gastrointestinal problem or a respiratory ailment, even if the initial tests are inconclusive.
- Do not rule out the possibility of a heart attack just because you are young, especially if you have risk factors such as smoking, hypertension, high blood pressure, obesity, or a family history of heart trouble.
- Assist your doctor in securing copies of any previous studies done to evaluate heart disease.

Recommendations: More specific recommendations include the following:

- Beware of the patient who seems too young to have the disease. Is it our own fear of mortality or our wish that these diseases only occur at the end of life that cause us to overlook cancer and heart disease in the under-50 age group?
- Pain and bleeding, although ubiquitous, are often serious symptoms. Consider the most serious diagnosis and rule it out.
- If you are not sure, refer!!! This gets harder under managed care, but so is missing diagnoses in unfamiliar areas.
- If you do not thoroughly understand all the presenting symptoms and clinical course of a disease, learn them quickly, and rule out serious disease or refer.
- If you have ordered diagnostic testing, understand their accuracy limits. Have a system to record and follow up results. Communicate results to your patient. COMMUNICATE!!!
- Defensive thinking and behavior are not necessarily bad for your patients. Failure to think of the worst diagnosis, failure to rule it out with appropriate testing, and failure to diagnose treatable disease are bad for your patients. In fact, it is best not to think of this behavior as "defensive medicine" but rather as "good medicine." The goal is to provide the best diagnostic care for your patients.

Chapter 4: Self-Assessment Checklist

1. Might you see cases of breast cancer, myocardial infarction, lung or colon cancer in your practice?
2. Do you usually disregard breast cancer as a diagnosis in premenopausal women because of their age?
3. When diagnosing female patients presenting with pain (but no lump) in their breasts, do you typically assume the pain is due to a cyst? If so, you might make the same mistake as did Ms B's internist in her case study.
4. Does your diagnosis of myocardial infarction rely heavily on the classic risk factors: age, weight, whether or not the patient smokes, and family history of heart problems?

5. When treating patients presenting with symptoms possibly relating to myocardial infarction, do you typically have the same index of suspicion for patients presenting in the office as for patients presenting in the emergency department?
6. When treating patients presenting with symptoms possibly relating to myocardial infarction, do you typically document all patient complaints relative to pain/pressure and its location?
7. When treating patients presenting with symptoms possibly relating to myocardial infarction, do you typically document persona and family history of heart disease?
8. When treating patients presenting with symptoms possibly relating to myocardial infarction, do you typically document the results of previous cardiac studies and compare them with any studies you have ordered?
9. When treating patients presenting with symptoms possibly relating to myocardial infarction, do you typically continue diagnostic testing (including a stress test) until the diagnosis is ruled out?
10. When treating patients presenting with symptoms possibly relating to colon cancer, do you typically refer for an endoscopic or barium examination?
11. If the examples in this chapter do not relate to your specialty, what are the "high risk" conditions in your specialty, what are the "high risk" conditions in your specialty? How are you managing your diagnosis-related risks with regard to these conditions?

Chapter Five

Minimizing The Risks of Miscommunication

In the chapter on diagnostic risk management, we discussed how reduced in patient stays and shortened office visits have impeded the physician's ability to use the traditional technique of observing the disease process over time to aid in diagnosis. This change has altered the physician's approach to diagnosis over the last 10 years in that diagnostic tests have been substituted for diagnostic observation. In a parallel shift, over the last decade, significant changes have also occurred in the area of physician communication.

In this chapter, we will examine the shifts in physician- patient communication and how those shifts have created new risks, threatening the quality of patient care and creating additional malpractice dangers. We will also examine other important communication risks in practice including those related to informed consent, communications with a patient's family, or even with other physicians. Throughout, we will provide recommendations for managing these risks, in an attempt to improve patient care and keep liability low.

Traditional Doctor-Patient Communication

Traditional societies, such as western European, have viewed medicine as a somewhat magical process. The physician-healer was in possession of this magic knowledge that he dispensed in small doses to each patient. The traditional images of the strong, silent American hero fed the image of the physician "taking care of his patients." In this quasiparental role, the physician was not expected to, nor did he feel the need to, explain his actions to patients. His charts were his property, not the patients'. His prescriptions, often written in Latin, preserved the secret magic code between physician and pharmacist. The physician healer was indeed "captain of the ship," responsible to no one except his conscience.

In this atmosphere, patients had little choice but to put their faith in physicians. "Faith," like "magic," implied a passive role for the patient, while the doctor battled with the forces of disease. Indeed, the patient was discouraged from asking questions, and rare was the physician who felt he had to explain his actions, even in cases with disastrous outcomes.

As recently as 30 years ago, in a tradition going back thousands of years, communication was unidirectional from patient to doctor. The carefully obtained and documented patient history was the backbone of diagnosis. Disease was to be sought out by looking for its natural course in the minutely documented history of the patient. In an era before computerized tomography (CT) scans, ultrasounds, magnetic resonance imaging (MRI), and endoscopies, the view inside the patient's body was through the patient's history.

Two major trends in the 1970s changed this perception of patient communication. The first trend diminished the importance of patient history, and the second trend challenged the passive role of the patient.

The Shift in Doctor-Patient Communication

In 1974, the development of the CT scan changed the approach to diagnosis. Although nuclear medicine had already been scanning patients for almost 10 years, it was CT scanning and the resultant publicity that convinced doctors and patients that, at last, we could see inside the human body relatively easily. No longer would patients and physicians have to observe the natural history of disease. They could look for disease directly. CT and ultrasound scanning opened almost all of the body to direct view.

Autopsies as the answer to disease became passé. And, in some ways, so did the patient's history and its accompanying physical examination. The hands-on magic touch of the physician, which for thousands of years had reassured patients, had begun to diminish. Machines began to replace the hands, ears, and eyes of the physician.

The second major shift of the 70s was the emergence of a class of patients who felt they had not fared well under the traditional system and were ready to revolt. Women of all ages gathered together in support groups and discussed their bodies, among other things. Our Body, Ourselves, a seminal self-help book for women published in Massachusetts, became the Uncle Tom's Cabin of the women's medical revolution.

Women challenged the notion that only physicians had the right to medical knowledge. Disenfranchised from the medical profession for centuries, they saw in their feminism a way to communicate knowledge to each other outside traditional medicine. They requested, indeed often demanded, to learn more from their doctors. No longer content to play a passive role in society, they refused to play a passive role in the doctor's office. As women demanded more information, their husbands and boyfriends did also. The magic of one-way physician communication had begun to evaporate.

If those of you who are under 45 think that this history presentation is too dramatic, ask your older colleagues about women in medicine before this revolution. There were few women in medical school before 1970, and many residency programs openly refused to take women. Taking away the one-way communication became an effective move for women wishing to introduce equality into the medical establishment.

The New Era of Doctor-Patient Communication

What is the impact of these two shifts 25 years later? Clearly, there has been a loss of some of the physician mystique that one-way communication fostered. Older physicians, of course, will have more trouble adjusting to this than younger ones, for whom this type of magic probably never existed.

One group of physicians may have particular trouble with this issue: physicians born and trained in other countries. These doctors, trained with more classical traditions, may find American patients "too pushy." If you come from this type of training, you must constantly fight the tendency to treat your patients in the traditional one-way communication mode. Such interaction will only frustrate American patients today, and, although you may not be able to discern it, this frustration will lead to lower levels of patient satisfaction with their medical care. On the other hand, younger U.S.-trained physicians will have less frustration operating in a two-directional communication environment. However, these physicians may not know how to use the mystique of one-way communication to their advantage: specifically, when dealing with patients who have immigrated from another country.

These patients, especially in large urban areas, have never experienced the communication revolution, and still expect their physicians to make all their decisions for them. "Whatever you say," is a common response as is, "You are the doctor." However, there are as many communication risks when encountering a docile patient as there are for more openly difficult patients. We will discuss communication risks generally in the next sections, leaving discussion on more difficult patients for the next chapter.

Managing Communication Risks

In today's medical environment, dominated by the patient's expectation of a two-way communication mode, there are more ways to mis-communicate than ever before. Ineffective communication with patients can lead to misdiagnoses, patient frustration, and even malpractice lawsuits.

Miscommunication with other physicians can lead also to delays and omissions in care, which also may bring liability. We will discuss physician-patient communication first and then address physician-physician communication.

Physician-Patient Communication

Communication between a physician and patients (or their families) is, by far, the leading communication problem in risk management. In fact, recent studies of all malpractice risks have demonstrated that communication breakdowns are the number-one factor leading to litigation, even more than a substandard result. Good communication is great medicine and greater risk management.

A recent study of 120 physician offices in Oregon and Colorado, demonstrated how important physician- patient communication is to quality patient care and how communication errors can lead to malpractice lawsuits.[28] The study, which analyzed communication behaviors of primary-care physicians and surgeons, separated physicians into "no claims" doctors (those with fewer than two malpractice claims filed against them) and "claims" doctors (those with more than two claims against them). Significant differences in communication behaviors of "no-claims" and "claims" physicians were identified in primary- care physicians, but not in surgeons.

Compared with "claims" physicians, "no-claims" primary-care physicians used more statements of orientation (educating patients about what to expect and the flow of a visit), laughed and used humor more, and tended to use more facilitation (soliciting patients' opinions, checking understanding, and encouraging patients to talk). "No-claims" physicians also spent more time on average in routine visits than did "claims" physicians (mean: 18.3 versus 15 minutes).13

Recommendations

1. At the outset of a patient examination, use orientating statements that help the patient develop appropriate expectations about the visit. "First I'll examine you and then we will talk the problem over" or "I will leave time for your questions" are both helpful.

2. During the examination, use facilitative comments to extract more and better information from the patient. Statements like "Go on, tell more about that" or opinion solicitors like "What do you think caused that to happen?" are extremely useful.

3. Do not assume that the same communication skills are appropriate for every specialty group.

In the above study, there was an insignificant difference between "claims" and "no-claims" surgeons. In your specialty literature, find out more about what types of communication skills are beneficial for your practice.

Assessing the Patient

The first critical step in managing communication risk with your patient is to assess your patient's psychosocial background and expected response. This is crucial if you are to avoid the common pitfalls leading to strained doctor-patient relationships and even liability. Although this assessment will be a challenge regardless of the patient's age or background, it is especially difficult with foreign-born patients who speak little or no English.

For example, the Southeast Asian immigrant patient is unlikely to ask you many questions. Your main challenge will be getting enough of an adequate history to even begin your workup. Not only will language be a problem, but the traditions of far eastern medicine are so different from traditional western approaches that even when the patient understands your English, you may be "speaking a different language." Consider the following case study:

This case demonstrates the absolute necessity of being able to have a meaningful two-way communication in order to glean an accurate patient history. What could the physicians here done differently? The most obvious answer is to have an interpreter available who can translate the patient's response into English. Best is a professional interpreter who also understands cultural nuances that may prevent the patient from accurately giving a history. Second best is a staff member or patient family member who can act an intermediary interpreter.

Case Study

A 37-year-old Southeast Asian man entered the emergency room with a classic presentation of RLQ pain, fever, and leukocytosis. In taking the history, the hospital personnel asked the patient if he had recently eaten. The patient misunderstood the question, saying "no" to what he thought was the question of whether he wanted something to eat. Exploratory surgery was begun 1 hour later. Unfortunately not only was a normal appendix found, but the patient aspirated during recovery. He developed a difficult-to-treat aspiration pneumonia. The surgeon, anesthesiologist, and hospital were all sued and were found liable for initiating surgery without adequate history and precautions to prevent aspiration.

Other Issues and Recommendations

What kind of language do you use in your practice? If it is the language of medical consultation, the patient or their family may not understand you. And if they do not, any adverse outcome of this lack of understanding may result in malpractice. This may be as easily proved as is the lack of informed consent. Especially when you are giving follow-up instructions, be sure you know and document what the patient understands.

If you work with bilingual or non-English speaking patients, have routine follow-up orders or instructions printed in the patient's language. The consultant report to the referring physician should be in English, but the letter to the patient should be in his or her first language if not English. Your consent forms in office or hospital should also be in the appropriate primary language.

Time Constraints on Communication

In today's busy practice environment, there is simply less time for each patient than there used to be. With less time for each patient, there is less time for real communication. It seems that, in most patient examinations, there is just enough time for information gathering. . . and barely enough for that. Given this time constraint, it becomes all the more imperative that you gather as much information as possible from the patient before you meet with him/her.

As your time is the most precious resource in your practice, you want to use it at maximal efficiency. As in any integrated process, the goal is to use the most precious resource most efficiently. In your office, this means doing as many jobs as possible before the key resource is used, so that resource can concentrate and deliver only the service that it is designed to provide. The most valuable resource in a doctor's office is the physician's time. As such, the challenge is to do as much of the generic information gathering from the patient as possible before you are called in, so that your time is spent asking the key medical questions and performing a physical examination.

By doing so, you will be able to review the answers to these more generic questions before meeting with the patient. You can then get a good idea of what the key issues are before even stepping in the room with the patient. This will allow you maximal "real communication" time in your consult. Ideally, you will take better histories and understand your patient's health much more thoroughly this way, without using any more of your time.

How do you achieve this efficiency? Answer the questions in the self-assessment checklist at the end of this chapter, and consider using our mock-up patient questionnaire that follows. These will give you the tools you will need to make your communications system more efficient.

Informed Consent

The second major challenge in managing communication risks continues to be securing adequate informed consent in surgical or diagnostic procedures. Despite the extensive risk management efforts over the past 15 years, this area still represents a significant portion of communication-related claims.

We suspect the fault in this area lies with individual physicians, not with the consent forms themselves. Not only should patients have witnesses to sign forms, the physician should make a separate chart note about explaining the procedure to the patient. Further, the physician should be absolutely certain that the patient understands what the physician is saying.

Physician liability in the area of informed consent often arises because the doctor fails to tell patients about treatment options other than the option for which he or she wants the patient's consent. In other cases, physicians are found liable when a spouse or other family member with a vested interest in the treatment of the patient is not made aware of the risks of a procedure or is not given other options of treatment. The following case study demonstrates both of these failures.

The surgeon made two mistakes in obtaining informed consent. First, he failed to ask the patient if he could involve the patient's husband in the discussions. This was a mistake not only in terms of informed consent but because of the husband's interest in the reproductive ability of his spouse. More generally, this was an error because, by leaving the husband out of the loop, the surgeon only increased the chances that the couple would be dissatisfied with her care. The surgeon also failed to provide the patient or her spouse with an explanation of other treatment options. As most states' informed consent laws require the physician to tell the patient about the benefits and risks of alternative treatments, this a common and potentially liability-creating mistake.

A new and potentially disturbing area of informed consent risk involves genetic testing. There are now a number of conditions, including colon cancer, that may have some identifiable genetic basis. It is extremely important that, if you are going to screen the patient for genetic disease, you obtain informed consent regarding these tests. Another vial of blood to the laboratory does not seem like much at the time. When the patient, however, finds out that he has been screened for genetic disease, and that those results are not only available to him but also to his employers or insurers at some point, he is bound to be angry. Anger, in many cases, leads to lawsuits.

There already have been a number of cases in which physicians have been sued for ordering unwanted tests, when the test results have influenced the socioeconomic status of the patient. This area will continue to grow over the next decade. Although physicians may believe that they are providing the best medicine for their patients, they must protect themselves by carefully explaining these procedures in advance (including the possible misuse of the information) and obtaining patients' prior written consent.

Recommendations: When obtaining patients' informed consent, make sure to do the following:

1. Have the consent form signed and witnessed.
2. Make sure that patients understand what they are signing.
3. Involve close family members/spouses, and make sure they understand the process as well.
4. Explain the benefits and risks of alternative treatments and diagnostic tests in addition to the one(s) you are recommending.
5. In deciding which risks to include in your discussion, explain all risks considered possible by your specialty. Read the literature, and be aware of what colleagues are explaining.
6. In deciding which alternatives to include in your discussion, explain those considered reasonable by your specialty. Read the literature, and be aware of what colleagues are including in their discussions.
7. Avoid the tendency to leave out explanatory discussion because you

think that patients will not understand it. It is better to assume that they will comprehend; you will be providing better care and have less risk of liability.

8. Be aware that informed consent laws apply not only to procedures, but also to prescription drugs. There is no need to get written consent for every prescription, but it is essential to explain drug risks, side effects, and contraindications. And make sure to note the discussion in the chart.

Case Study

Surgeon Jack Confidant saw a 28-year-old woman with a history of excessive vaginal bleeding. He believed that the patient required a hysterectomy, and he clearly explained the procedure to her. He did not, however, involve her husband in the conversations, and he never discussed other treatment options (such as medications).

The operation proceeded smoothly and there were no postoperative complications. Months later, the patient sued successfully for defectively authorized surgery even though there were no complications. The courts upheld the claim of damages on the basis of lack of total information in the informed consent.

Physician-to-Physician Communication

A third area of communication risk relates to correspondence between physicians. The most common scenario resulting in mistakes in patient care (and often in liability) is where one partner fails to transmit information to a covering partner. This may be a risk for you. Ask yourself the following:

- Do you have a well-defined mechanism of transferring patient information to the partners in your office and in the hospital?
- When you receive information from another physician, do you read it, or do you rely on a verbal summary from your colleague?
- If you do not get along with a referring physician, do you tend to not listen to him/her? If so, it is that much more important that you read his/her notes carefully.
- Are the reports of referring physicians or partners legible and understandable

to you? Sometimes or always?

- Are your reports likely to be understood by other doctors? Sometimes or always?
- Do you get the information you need from other physicians promptly, or is there a delay because their reports are dictated ? Do you think you are holding up other doctors this way?

The following case study demonstrates the risks of physician-physician communication.

Case Study

Dr. Sheila Goldstone was leaving for her vacation Saturday afternoon as soon as she completed her hospital rounds. Mr. Shiffer, a 60-year-old man with a history of cardiac failure, complained of mild nausea and increasing abdominal pain. Leaving a note in the chart concerning his new symptoms, Dr. Goldstone paged her partner Bob Roberts, who was covering for the group on the weekend. Bob was swamped with two new admissions, but promised to check on Mr. Shiffer later that day. Bob was not as concerned with Mr. Shiffer's condition at 4 PM as Sheila had been, but he put in a request for a surgical consult.

Unfortunately, no one on call for surgery followed up on the request. The floor coordinator was out sick, and the head nurse had two floors to cover. At 9 AM, a general surgeon did see Mr. Shiffer and diagnosed small bowel obstruction with perforation. His condition continued to deteriorate, and he died after surgery.

Lawyers for Mr. Shiffer's estate successfully argued that both internists were responsible for the delay in diagnosis and treatment leading to his death.

Dr. Goldstone's failure to impress upon her partner the potential seriousness of the situation resulted in Dr. Roberts not following up with the surgeon. Dr. Goldstone's particular high level of concern here should have been communicated to Dr. Roberts. A routine note or mention to your colleague may not be a strong enough communication when you are concerned about preventing a potential emergency.

Recommendation: Consider a "Level of Concern" grading system for communications to other clinicians who are covering your patients: "A" for highest priority (high risk patients), "B" for average priority, and "C" for lower priority.

Chapter 5: Self-Assessment Checklist

How does your communication appear to your patients? To answer this question, you might consider hiring actors or interns to "act" as patients as then videotape your interactions.

If you are a golfer, swimmer, or tennis player, you must be aware of the techniques of videotaping your physical motions to improve your skills. It is hard to know what your golf stroke looks like and correct your problems, without seeing yourself on tape. Think about applying the same approach to your patient communication skills. With video camera costs so low, you might easily install one in your consultation room and use actors or real patients (if their informed consent is given). Then at your leisure, view the tapes with either a close friend or spouse, preferably someone not in the medical field.

When analyzing the tape, ask yourself: How do you present yourself? Can you be understood? What about your choice of words, tone of voice? Do you appear rushed or disinterested? Do you appear sympathetic or insensitive? How is your body language? Do you make eye contact with your patient? Do you smile and nod appropriately?

To improve efficiency in information gathering, so as to free your time and improve doctor-patient communication, consider the following questions:

1. Do your new patients fill out questionnaires in advance before you see them?

2. Does your office staff help?

3. Could you automate the information-gathering process? Many adults today are used to computer questions on a screen, ATM style.

4. Could you save 5 minutes of each patient visit by collecting information in your waiting room and have it printed before you see each patient?

5. Could insurance questions be incorporated into each visit questionnaire? In this era of managed care, patients have more of these questions for the doctors than ever.

6. Do you give out pamphlets on common ailments in the waiting rooms for patients to read before your examination? Many of these are available from national specialty societies.

7. Do you have a separate viewing room where patients could watch videotapes explaining procedures or treatments so they become educated before meeting with you?

Chapter Six

Managing High-Risk Communication Areas

In a clinician's practice, there are a number of areas in which strong communication skills are especially important. Communication failures in these circumstances are either particularly common or extraordinarily dangerous in terms of patient care and/or malpractice. In this chapter, we will address a number of common high-risk communication areas including how to handle troublesome patients, how to discuss bad outcomes, and how to communicate effectively in the single patient encounter.

Communicating With Difficult Patients

One of the greatest challenges facing the clinician is to communicate with difficult patients in a way that fosters accurate diagnosis and facilitates quality treatment. Unfortunately, there is no one way to deal with difficult patients, probably because there are so many types of difficult patients. In this section, we will address four common types of difficult patients and how to communicate with them to improve their care and limit liability.

The Disruptive Patient

Disruptive patients are always a risk-management problem. Particularly with violent patients or patients under the influence of alcohol or drugs, it is essential that you and your staff have a protocol for dealing with the situation. Although violence may only be a real concern in emergency departments, a disruptive patient can present anywhere, as the following case study demonstrates.

Case Study

Mrs. Solvay was in treatment for renal failure for several years in New York. When her son- in-law and daughter were transferred to Los Angeles, she moved to California to be near them. She was referred to a dialysis

> center in Los Angeles near her new home. A difficult and demanding patient who was ill at ease in her new surroundings, she disrupted the entire facility upon each visit. The staff tried to calm her each time, as did the physician who spoke to her sympathetically.
>
> After a few months, there was little change in her behavior. The physician again warned her that her behavior may result her in no longer being welcome at his office. He noted all discussions with her in the chart. She acted out again at her next visit. The other patients and staff were so upset that the supervising nephrologist refused to treat her further. She then sued for abandonment, although he had referred her to another center.
>
> The court found for the physician, saying the woman's own actions caused the breakdown of the physician-patient relationship. Therefore, there was no abandonment. The court noted that not only had the physician repeatedly warned her and given her 6 weeks' notice of discharge, but had referred her to another center.

This case illustrates a number of tactics for dealing with a disruptive patient. One should communicate sympathetically with the patient, to try to curb the behavior at the outset, as the physician did in this case. Often, these patients are seeking attention. A positive talk by staff, or better yet, the physician, can prevent problems. Sterner warnings are appropriate when the patient continues with disruptive behavior. The patient's disruptive behavior and concomitant discussions should be noted in the patient's chart. This is an invaluable tool in a defense against any claim the patient may later bring forth.

Also, it should be noted that in a critical situation (as in the case of a dialysis patient above, where discontinuation of care is life-threatening), when referring a patient to another center, the other center needs to acknowledge acceptance of the patient. Otherwise, patient abandonment could still be alleged.

The Patient Who Refuses Treatment

The best strategy for dealing with these patients is to clearly communicate to them the risks and benefits of refusing the treatment at hand; then note the discussion in the chart. Better yet, follow our recommendations in the last chapter on informed consent, and get the patient to sign a form indicating his/her refusal. (See a sample form in the self-assessment checklist.) Also, with the patient's consent, involve spouse or family members, if possible.

The same principles and recommendations apply for dealing with the patient who insists on leaving the hospital against your advice. Disclose all risks, document the discussion in the chart, and have the patient sign the hospital's "signed out against medical advice" form.

The Doubting Patient

Often, the patients who become most combative in the final analysis are not so difficult at the outset. The patient who does not refuse treatment or testing, but who subtly doubts or questions your choices, may be the one who ends up suing you for malpractice. How do you recognize these "doubting patients?"

The patients who overtly ask for a second opinion are the least difficult. Simply send that patient to another physician, preferably a specialist, for a second opinion. If you do not, and there is anything less than a perfect outcome, you will be a ripe target for malpractice action.

Other doubting patients will not be so obvious in their suspicions. You may have to read between the lines of their conversation and interpret their body language as well. For example, a patient or her family member may ask you if she should see a specialist (or another type of specialist). Your first response may be to calm the patient and family and reassure them that you see and treat this type of condition all the time. Even though this response may be justifiable (you may well see and treat this condition routinely), your competence is not the issue here.

What this patient/family member may be trying to tell you is that they prefer to see a specialist (or another type of specialist). Whether or not you believe the patient really needs the referral, try to make it happen. Although this may be more difficult in managed-care settings, a referral is good patient care and smart risk management.

The Patient with Last-Second Recollection

Those physicians who deal with elderly people will recognize the phenomena of the last-minute patient recollection of a major problem after you have almost completed the visit. When Columbo, the TV detective, asked questions as he was apparently leaving, the person to whom the question was addressed was caught off guard. In your office, when the patient is rushing out the door, it is you who are caught off guard.

Faced with this situation, you have two alternatives: either you delay their exit and further stretch your schedule, or you brush off the question with a quick answer. The delay costs you time, aggravation, and staff salaries. The quick answer may cost you patient confidence and a lawsuit demonstrated by the following case study.

Case Study

Mrs. Costa, a 75-year-old widow, gets so nervous about her visits to each of her many doctors, that she frequently forgets why she goes in the first place. Rather than writing down her chief complaints in advance, she tries to remember everything during her appointment with Dr. Caswell, her internist. On her last visit, she remembers a low-grade pain between her shoulder blades, just as she is leaving. Dr. Caswell gets a phone call as Mrs. Costa is describing the pain. He reassures her it is probably just a pulled muscle and that she shouldn't worry about it.

As the pain increases over the next few days, Mrs. Costa is concerned but remembers that Dr. Caswell had reassured her not to worry. After 3 days the pain grows much worse, and she calls the rescue squad; who take her to a local emergency room. She is admitted after a CT scan shows a dissecting aortic aneurysm, and she dies 2 days later.

This case demonstrates the difficulty of dealing with the last-second recollection. Dr. Caswell did not take the time to consider Mrs. Costa's final complaints about the pain in her back. He was too rushed to take these last-second statements seriously. This, unfortunately, turned out to be a tragic mistake.

Recommendation: One technique that may alleviate this problem is to ask patients as they enter your examination room, "How can I help you?" This is a nonthreatening approach that usually elicits the patient's real chief complaint. Once the patient is finished talking, you can control the remainder of the allotted time for history and physical examination.

Communicating Bad Outcomes

Communicating bad outcomes to patients is one of the most difficult tasks a physician must perform. Perhaps in part because it so difficult, many clinicians communicate poorly with patients and their families after a bad outcome. Another contributing factor to the miscommunication after bad outcomes has been the advice of risk managers of a previous era.

Classical risk-management teaching had advocated that the less said about a bad outcome to anyone, the better. Insurance companies, lawyers, and hospital risk managers had all been trained to keep any problems very quiet. Only behind closed doors, with certain qualified individuals, were you allowed to discuss the case. "Not even with your partners or colleagues" you were warned. Did all of this secrecy really make sense? Did it improve patient relations or prevent litigation? No.

Today's risk-management approach to dealing with poor outcomes is to communicate with the patient and family directly and sympathetically, as soon after the outcome as possible. Although many risk managers still insist on avoiding an apology in all situations, there may be instances when you believe that one is appropriate. If so, use language that shows an acknowledgment of the reality of regret and tragedy ("I am sorry that this happened" or "I am sorry that you are in such pain") rather than language that shows an acknowledgment of malfeasance or wrongdoing. Beyond this, consider the following recommendations when communicating bad outcomes to patients and their families.

Recommendations

- When things go wrong, or you suspect a patient is unhappy, do not give in to the natural inclination to avoid him/her or his/her family. Rather, give the patient as much time as he/she wants. A genuine interest in trying to resolve problems and create the best treatment plan going forward should be your attitude. Patients will forgive honest mistakes, and your extra time and concern can turn any situation in your favor.
- In communicating with patients and family, direct sympathetic phrasing is best. Consider something like this: "I am sorry that you have suffered complications. These are the problems we are facing, and here is our plan." Of course, proper eye contact and other body language is essential in communicating a sympathetic yet strong image.
- In meeting with patients and family after a bad outcome, do not bring attorneys or other risk- management officials. The meeting should be about building bridges and healing pain. However, if potential claimants request bringing an attorney, you should also have legal representation.

Communicating in the Single Encounter

The single encounter with a patient provides an atmosphere in which the clinician may get only one chance to be "right" or to make an appropriate diagnosis. In this situation, the stakes are much higher, as is this risk of miscommunication. Although the single encounter is common emergency department practice, the scenario also occurs in other types of practices. Does it occur in your practice? Does it occur during a new patient visit? During a phone consultation? During an outpatient clinic or emergency room visit?

Recommendation: To maximize patient care and for liability protection in one-time encounters, documentation is critical. You must document not only what you did observe in the patient, but what you also did not observe. Further, make sure to note what you told the patient or family about follow-up and what you found or did not find on physical examination, x-ray examination, or laboratory tests. Also document the existence of a referral, if applicable. Although documentation is always critical to proper risk management, it is especially so in the high-risk single-encounter situation.

Chapter 6: Self-Assessment Checklist

Disruptive Patients

Consider making a thorough analysis of your interactions with disruptive patients. After any confrontational interaction, write down your notes immediately. Ask yourself the following.

1. Is your behavior with disruptive patients appropriate?
2. Do you become angry or uncommunicative?
3. We all know how we act in conflict with spouses and children. Do you behave differently in your patient-centered conflicts?
4. Are you making your patients into difficult patients?
5. Is your office user-friendly? Are there enough seats and reading material for patients kept waiting? Do you have a television set or a coffee pot? Would a personalized computer interview screen not only give you needed information, but keep your patients occupied and happy? Are your gowns large enough? Does your receptionist smile or frown? Do you stick to your schedule?
6. If your patients know they are on a prepaid plan, do they see you as just as wanting to get them out the door? There is more and more being written in the lay press about capitation. How would you feel about being

a capitated patient in your practice? Recent popular magazine articles are giving instructions to patients about how to trap physicians in managed-care guidelines. Could this be a problem for you? "The satisfied patient rarely sues, but a dissatisfied one will find a reason to."

7. When you and your patients have conflicting values, how do you handle this? Are you psychologically and professionally prepared to discharge a patient? Do you have a written plan? If not, even verbal conflicts can escalate into lawsuits. If you are going to discharge a patient, make sure that you are giving him or her enough time and notice to find another physician and consider abandonment issues, especially if a critical illness is involved. Have a policy for forwarding charts.

The Patient Who Refuses Treatment

Use the form on the following page for a patient who refuses treatment. It could save you a malpractice lawsuit down the road.

REFUSAL TO UNDERGO TREATMENT

Name ______________________________

Age ______________________________

Date ______________________________

Location ______________________________

Dr. ____________________ has explained to me in detail the foreseeable risks associated with a ____________________, and I have elected not to undergo a ____________________.

Dr. ____________________ has explained to me in detail that the foreseeable risks associated with my electing not to undergo a ____________________ are ____________________________.

____

Patient Date

____

Legal Representative (if patient cannot understand)

____

Witness Date

Chapter Seven

Managing the Dangers of Drug Therapy

In analyzing the risk of medication errors, we rely heavily of the seminal 1993 study of medication errors published by the PIAA.[29] In that study, close to 400 cases of claimed liability based on medication error were reviewed. All these cases were selected to represent indemnity payouts of at least $5,000.

By 1998–1999, other studies from the Institute of Medicine and Harvard Medical Practice Study claimed that medication errors were the leading cause of medical injury accounting for more than 19% of total injuries system wide.[30] A JAMA article in 1997 estimated that in 1997 the total cost of drug related morbidity and mortality exceed $136 billion.[31]

Patients claiming damages in the 1993 study were not particularly different from those in the other studies that we examined. As in the other studies, the ages of the patients claiming injury were younger than clinicians might expect. Here, the average age of the patient was 42 years, with women predominating at all ages. More than 60% of all claimants in this study were under age 50. Furthermore, in terms of liability, 75% of all dollars paid out were in the under-50 age group.

Type and Level of Injury

The level of injury claimed in these cases was high. More than 42% of the cases involved significant permanent injury, and fully 20% resulted in death. Naturally, these two categories had the highest payouts, accounting for 79% of all monies paid.

The most common complications among multiple categories were central nervous system (CNS) injuries, accounting for 15% of the total. Predominant drugs involved were narcotics and tranquilizers. Allergy and cutaneous complications together accounted for 20% of the total, with antibiotics and topical medications being the leading offenders.

Cardiac, respiratory and bleeding complications accounted for another 25% of the total, with the drugs primarily being narcotics, respiratory agents, anticoagulants, and antihypertensive agents. All other categories of complications accounted for the rest. There was no consistent correlation between the most common offending drug and the most common type of injury or complication.

Drug Type

In the 1993 study, the two classes of drugs involved in most claims were antibiotics and glucocorticoids. Together, these accounted for 23% of all cases and 27% of all dollars paid out. The next grouping of analgesics, nonsteroidal anti-inflammatory drugs/acetylsalicylic acid (NSAID/ASA) topicals, accounted for an additional 25% of all claims and 19% of all dollars. These five categories are significant because virtually all physicians, whether generalists or specialists, have frequent occasions to prescribe these drugs. Therefore, every physician should be aware of the risk for complications.

The following are the leading complications for the five most liability-producing types of drugs:

Antibiotics

1. Failure to note documented allergies
2. Not using the most appropriate drug
3. Drug inappropriate for medical condition

Glucocorticoids

1. Incorrect dosage
2. Failure of communication
3. Failure to monitor side effects

Narcotics

1. Drug inappropriate for medical condition
2. Incorrect dosage
3. Failure to monitor for side effects

NSAIDS/NSA

1. Inadequate medical history
2. Failure to note documented allergies
3. Failure to monitor side effects

Topicals, Dermatologics, Ophthalmologics

1. Incorrect dose
2. Failure of communication between physician and patient
3. Drug inappropriate for medical condition

More recently the "white paper " on medication errors from PIAA in 2000 categorized additional drugs as HIGH ALERT.[32] These are INSULIN, POTASSIUM CHLORIDE CONCENTRATE, NARCOTICS and ANTICOAGULANTS.

In addition that white paper cited errors in prescribing drugs with similar names, a problem that exacerbated in the 90's and 00s' with the explosion of new drugs and the lack of original names for them. Consider the drugs Celebrex®, Cerebyx® and Celexa®, different drugs, very different indications. Be very specific and clear not only as to the drug you are prescribing but also the condition you are prescribing for.

Many hospitals have very specific guidelines for using abbreviations, so that orders are not confused by their nurses. Consider using these guides in your office as well. Spell out abbreviations where possible

Use a leading zero (0) before a decimal in your prescribing , such as 0.5 instead of .5

DO NOT use a trailing zero, as this may increase the dose by TEN times if not read correctly.

The PIAA study does not mention the potential dangers of writing prescriptions for drugs outside your area of expertise: both in terms of mishaps in patient care and liability. In addition to patient lawsuits, state and federal agencies are keeping a careful watch on the prescribing patterns of specialists who ordinarily would not use certain classes of drugs in their practice. Like casual or social medical advice (discussed in previous chapters), casual prescription writing to friends or family can be a problem.

Some states have gone so far as to forbid from writing any prescription for family members or anyone else with whom they do not have a formal documented doctor-patient relationship. The state attorney general's office may suspend your license or your ability to write any prescription if abuse is suspected. Do not think that you are immune if you order medications for yourself or your family from national mail-order supply houses. Their subscriber lists are periodically reviewed by the Drug Enforcement Administration for patterns of so-called abuse. You may risk even civil and criminal penalties if you cannot document standard- of-care performance in this area.

Physicians Involved

As could be predicted from the drug classes named, primary-care physicians were most often sued, accounting for 60% of all claims and equally divided between internal medicine and family practice. Gynecologists and pediatricians were involved much less often, at about 5% each. Also, at 3% to 5% total claim level were orthopedists, general surgeons, psychiatrists, and dermatologists. All other groups were at 2% or below. Emergency medicine physicians only represented 1% of all cases in the study, and their average loss of $25,000 was the lowest of all specialties.

Physicians, although the most common defendant (70%), were not the only parties sued. Nurses accounted for 13% of the total and pharmacists 8%. Covering or consulting physicians were sued 5% of the time. If you have an office nurse, show her/ him these figures. Better yet, write to the PIAA for a copy of the report. Your staff will benefit from this education.

Consider the following case study that demonstrates the potential dangers involved with the delivery of medications in a borderline case.

Case Study

Mrs. B is a 40-year-old legal secretary with a history of migraine headaches for which she was being treated by a neurologist. When her current medication ran out, she called the neurologist, who was in the midst of busy afternoon office hours. This particular medication comes in two dosage strengths. The physician, not checking her chart, told his office nurse to renew her medication at the higher strength.

Mrs. B refilled her prescription at a local branch of a large pharmaceutical chain. The new pharmacist on duty did not pick up the change in dosage when he filled the prescription.

When she returned home, Mrs. B noticed that the pills she received were different from the ones she usually took. She called the pharmacy and was told by the same pharmacist that the pills are a generic brand, probably from a different company than her usual brand. He reassured her that she had the correct pills.

Over the next week, Mrs. B got continually weaker, with a few near-fainting episodes. She visited her internist, who found her blood pressure to be extremely low. There was no history of change in her diet, medication, or general health to account for this.

Three days later, Mrs. B passed out at work and was taken to the hospital as an emergency admission. Her workup revealed no definite abnormality. When the internist checked her hospital chart against his office records, he realized what had happened.

In this case, the pharmacist could be held liable for failing to pick up the change in dosage. But what about the internist? His first mistake was that he called in the wrong order. He tried to go by memory without checking Mrs. B's chart. Further, when Mrs. B came in for the second visit, he again did not check the medication. He should have had Mrs. B bring in her old prescription to examine it.

Recommendations

To prevent against the common liability-producing errors demonstrated in this chapter, follow this list of recommendations:

- Note all prescriptions and refills on flow sheets.
- Avoid abbreviations, double check name and spelling of drug
- Clearly note allergies on the chart.
- Get good medication history.
- Use the Physicians' Desk Reference (PDR), or equivalent, regularly.
- Use written as well as oral instructions.
- Consider informed consent for drugs with potential side effects.
- Monitor narcotic use carefully, and monitor side effects.
- Keep careful records, especially for controlled substances.
- Have patients bring in medications they are currently taking.

Learn about recalls and new medication. Caution patients about pitfalls of ordering on-line.

Be careful about dosages in pediatrics and in the elderly, particularly if your elderly patients are small or frail. Most dosage recommendations are based on average size adults.

Chapter 7: Self-Assessment Checklist

1. Do you routinely note all prescriptions on flow sheets? Sometimes? Always?
2. Do you routinely take a thorough allergy history on all new patients?
3. Do you have a special section on your charts for allergies?
4. Do you routinely take a thorough medication history on all new patients?
5. Do you ask new patients to bring all current medications with them to your first examination?
6. Do you ask established patients to bring all current medications with them to in-office examinations?
7. Do you routinely use the PDR when prescribing or inquiring about patients' other medications?
8. Do you have a PDR in the examination room to save time in your research/prescription writing?
9. Do you have the new PDR computer? If you write many prescriptions in your practice, this device might save you time and aggravation.

Chapter Eight

Nonmedical Liability Risks for the Practicing Physician

Most physicians spend much of their time concerned about (and, ideally, working to prevent) medical malpractice claims. Although this concern is certainly justified, what doctors do not realize is that the every- day risks common to any operating business can also be a source of considerable liability. Like any small business owner, the practicing physician must endure the "triple threat of business liability."

This "triple threat" consists of the following: (1) lawsuits from your employees (age, race, or gender discrimination; sexual harassment; or wrongful termination); (2) lawsuits brought against your employees or partners for harassment, injury, or even violation of consumer collection laws; and (3) claims brought by patients and other visitors to your practice due to personal injuries occurring on premises or involving practice equipment and vehicles.

Reducing Liability to Your Employees and Staff

These days are treacherous for employee lawsuits. With Congress and state legislatures expanding the rights of employees, juries handing out excessive awards as a matter of routine, and unscrupulous lawyers feeding the litigation fire, employers have good reason to be worried. More employees will sue their bosses in the next decade than did workers in the past three decades combined! And physicians are no exception to this trend.

Sexual harassment, race discrimination, wrongful termination, violation of the Americans with Disabilities Act, age discrimination, running afoul of federal Medicare fraud provisions, HIPAA, gender discrimination, EEOC violations, breach-of-employment contract, and mismanagement of staff pension fund can all be grounds for a potentially devastating lawsuit. Although this is beyond the scope of this monograph, we implore you to find out more about employee lawsuits and how to avoid them through proper human resource policies.

Reducing Liability of Your Employees and Staff

The behavior of employees and staff can be time bombs ticking away in your office. Without proper employee policies, these time bombs could explode with possibly ruinous results both in terms of patient care and in lawsuit liability.

Under the law, you, your practice, and your partners can be held legally and financially responsible for the behavior of your employees. Further, even if staff members are not your employees, you may be held responsible if they acted under your direction in a clinic or hospital. More important, patients will include their judgment of your staff in how they evaluate your medical care (and whether or not they recommend you to others). For these reasons, it is essential that you institute policies that minimize the risk of staff misbehavior.

The Unqualified Employee Who Gives Medical Advice

One family practitioner was recently sued when one of her receptionists told a patient to take Anacin instead of aspirin, not realizing that Anacin contains aspirin. The patient, who was already taking an anticoagulant, developed gastrointestinal bleeding and was later admitted to the hospital. She also ended up suing the physician for malpractice.

Unfortunately, this type of situation occurs quite often. Assistants who hear common complaints from patients take notice of the diagnoses and treatments prescribed by their physician-bosses. In an effort to "not waste the doctor's time" on routine questions, these assistants sometimes will make quick recommendations to patients. Although these recommendations may be harmless and correct advice most of the time, whenever there is a problem (either due to wrong advice or a misinterpretation of the advice by the patient), you, as the physician, will be held responsible.

Recommendation: Make sure your nonmedical staff members never give medical advice under any circumstances. Be clear in your policy/employee manual, and make sure your employees understand.

The Employee Who Files Reports Before You've Read Them

Even when modern information management systems are put into place in medical offices, it is the staff that must make the system work. Often staffers are too eager to get all reports filed, forgetting that the physician must see the reports to ensure proper patient care and follow-up. Take heed from the following case:

As this case indicates, the mishandling of information — test results or other — can be extremely hazardous. Investigate how your support staff would have handled this situation. Could the mishap that occurred in Dr. W's take place in yours? Do you have a rule or procedure that ensures that this mistake is avoided?

Case Study

Dr. W sent patient Pete for a full range of laboratory work and a chest x-ray film as part of his physical examination. All the laboratory tests came back negative a few days later, and Dr. W had an assistant call Pete to give him the news. A second office assistant filed the x-ray film report, which came in 2 days after the laboratory reports. The x-ray film indicated a probable malignancy in the right lung. The x-ray report was not shown to Dr. W but instead was filed so Dr. W would see it at the follow-up appointment

There was no follow-up appointment. Pete thought that when all the tests were negative, he did not need to come back into the office. It was not until a year later, when Dr. W was served with a court summons, that he opened Pete's file and saw the x-ray film report. Meanwhile, Pete had been diagnosed with metastatic lung cancer and was suing Dr. W for missing the diagnosis.

Recommendation: Establish this simple rule for all employees: Never have them file any piece of information— even if they are "sure" the doctor will see it prior to the patient's next visit — if it does not have the physician's initials on it.

The Staffer Who Fails to Document Patient Contacts

Over the years, in part because of emergence of risk- management teachings, physicians have become better at documenting their communications with patients. We have emphasized the point repeatedly in this monograph. However, documentation is just as important for medical office employees. As we have stressed, chart notes of all patient contacts not only improve patient care (by preserving valuable knowledge about the patient's history), but also serve an invaluable service if your care is ever called into question later, in a malpractice suit or otherwise.

Recommendation: Make sure that staffers understand that every patient contact should be recorded in the patient's records. Yellow stick-on notes will not do, as they fall off too easily. All the information from each contact should end up in the file every time. Allow no exceptions.

Reducing Liability From the Medical Office Premises

Here, the third element of the "triple threat" will be examined: lawsuit dangers emerging from the medical office premises; that is, "premises liability." Although the discussion will be focused primarily on lawsuits brought by patients and other visitors to your medical office, these problems are also common sources of claims by employees in the form of lawsuits or worker's compensation claims. Thus, by following the recommended strategies, you can not only lower your exposure to outside lawsuits, but reduce your costs of worker's compensation or insurance premiums as well.

NOTE: Do not think, because the terms property owner and landowner are used here, that you are not at risk because you lease or otherwise rent your office premises. The law imposes premises liability on persons who lease property as it does for property owners.

The Legal Test

Like any other public accommodation, your office must be a "reasonably safe" premises "under the circumstances." What is "reasonable" under any set of circumstances, of course, is open to interpretation and argument. Although no physician (or any other property owner, for that matter) has the absolute duty to ensure the safety of his guests, he cannot ignore the issue entirely. In fact, the duty of care required of property owners varies with the circumstances, so it is often difficult to determine just how much attention to premises is enough.

In the end, the question of whether or not you are found to be liable for any injury at your office will center on four questions: What type of hazard caused the injury in question? How obvious was the hazard? How long had it existed before actions (if any) to prevent injury were taken? Were the precautions reasonable under the circumstances?

Once again, we are faced with the "reasonable under the circumstances" language: the type of gray area that frustrates nonlawyers and gives fodder to both sides of any legal debate. As physicians, we are particularly vulnerable to this inquiry because the guests on our premises are often persons most susceptible to injury: children, the infirm, the elderly. As such, we will be held to an extraordinarily high standard of care. What are reasonable precautions for many business owners may be inadequate in our circumstances.

The Scope of the Threat

In a 1991 closed-case study performed by the Risk Management Foundation (RMF) of the Harvard Medical Institutions, Inc., fully 15% of all claims managed by the foundation over a 14-year period were cases involving patient falls.[33] Although the majority of these cases accounted for relatively minor losses, the growth of large-verdict slip-and-fall cases in recent years indicate that the costs associated with patient falls can be significant. Fall-related claims can put a strain on valuable time and resources that are needed to address other more severe risk areas.

The Harvard RMF study also demonstrated a number of trends associated with medical office slip-and- fall cases, including the following high risk factors:

1. A patient older than 65 years
2. A patient with altered mental status
3. Substances on the office floor
4. Malfunctioning equipment
5. Assistance with mobility by a member of the staff

Further, the Harvard RMF study found that injuries occurred most often in the following areas (in order of frequency):

1. Patient's room
2. Halls and lobbies
3. Patient's bathroom
4. Radiology examination area
5. Emergency treatment areas

Do you see the high risk-factors and high-frequency injury areas in your practice? If you do, you are especially at risk for slip-and-fall lawsuits. Even if you do not, the premises liability danger is still an important risk to guard against, especially when you can reduce much of your risk by simply paying attention to a small number of potentially hazardous areas.

"Walking Around Knowledge" Required

The most important step you can take to reduce your premises liability risk is to gain some "walking around" knowledge of your office: that is making inspections of your office at regular intervals. These inspections should be made by you and your staff as well. In fact, all physicians and staff should make regular inspection of key patient areas, making notes for potential hazards. Simply by making inspections part of your operational routine, you will do much to highlight potential problems before they become hazardous.

Beyond this general rule, there are a number of key areas that are potential hazards in any office. The following list highlights the most important risk areas and suggests ways to improve safety and reduce the chance of a slip and fall injury and lawsuit.

Access Problem

Patients should be able to negotiate the office and its surroundings easily and safely. A slip/fall in the entrance of the office is one of the most common liability- producing scenarios. The usual culprits: slippery floors, carpet in disrepair, or faulty doors.

Recommendation: Walkways should be level and in good repair; doors should open easily; and stairwells should have adequate handrails. Always check carpets for disrepair or floors for wet areas. Nonskid matting is always a wise idea in office entrances, especially in areas of the country where wet or snowy weather is common.

Many potential hazards, such as wet floors, should be corrected immediately in order to avoid liability. The inquiry of how soon the landowner acted to prevent injury is one of the questions asked in the legal test for liability. Office staff should be trained not only to make routine inspections of the entrance and other high-risk areas, but also to order or make easy repairs immediately. There is nothing that juries and judges look down upon more than the situation in which the landowner sees one person injured by a hazard and does nothing before a second person is also injured by the same hazard.

The importance of using of signs to warn patients of potential hazards cannot be overstated. Here, this may mean "slippery when wet" and "wet floor" signs and other portable barriers to redirect traffic away from hazardous areas. In other areas, this may mean "Staff Only: No Admittance" signs or even cones and tape to block off restricted areas. In short, the investment you make in warning signs and portable barriers will pay for itself many times over in prevented injuries and claims.

Medical Equipment and Biohazardous Waste Problem

Consider the following hypothetical case study involving equipment and waste:

> **Case Study**
>
> In your medical office laboratory, the young son of one of your female patients was left unattended while the phlebotomist drew the patient's blood. The child, meanwhile, had climbed quietly up onto the counter and began reaching for the bright red sharps container. Before long, the boy got to the container and began playing with the needles. While the phlebotomist soon realized what was going on, and rushed the boy away from the container, it could have been too late.

In this case study, if the child was infected with HIV, hepatitis, or any other communicable disease, your liability could be enormous. This case study also demonstrates not only the importance of monitoring children in your office (discussed later), but also the need for safeguards around dangerous medical equipment and materials.

Recommendation: Biohazardous waste cannot be stored in patient-care areas or other high-traffic sites. Further, waste containers used in examination and treatment rooms must be secured to prevent spillage and keep out inquisitive patients and guests. If gas cylinders are used in the office, they should be stored and secured properly. Electrical equipment should be inspected regularly and should never be used when not functioning properly. Sharps, medications, and other potentially hazardous materials should be stored away from patients' access and locked away, if appropriate.

Driveways and Parking Lots Problem

Although cases have held that driveways and parking lots are not inherently dangerous areas, physicians are still routinely held responsible when patients are injured in their parking lots. Consider the case in which a woman entered a physician's office to make a phone call for emergency car service. She was not even a patient. When the woman left the office, walking through the doctor's lot, she was hit by a car. Allegedly, the car was driven by a patient, although no one stopped, and the driver was never identified. The injured woman sued the doctor, and the physician's comprehensive liability policy ultimately paid on the claim.

Recommendation: Drives should be well marked with arrows and signs. The views in the lot should be unobstructed by landscaping. One-way traffic flow is also a wise idea, as are speed bumps or dips.

Children Problem

Injuries to children are an ever-increasing source of lawsuits against landowners of all types. As the case study showed, you must be concerned with injuries to children, especially if you often have children as patients or in your waiting rooms. General practitioners, pediatricians, and gynecologists are most severely at risk.

The most common type of claim brought on behalf of children is the typical injury due to an accident that causes fracture or lacerations. However, injuries can be severe (electrocution, paralyzation).

Recommendation: Maintain the office as explained above; child-proof the office (covering electric outlets, using child-proof locks on closets, etc.); train staff to be particularly aware of children's whereabouts and behavior; and use signs and warnings to alert adults that they, not you, are responsible for their children's behavior and/or injuries. A "play at your own risk" sign is always a good idea.

Bathroom Problem

Bathrooms are a common source of liability, especially for physicians with elderly patients. The two major liability factors for injuries occurring in bathrooms are design and maintenance. Although maintenance of a safe bathroom is fairly straightforward, consider the problem of a faulty bathroom design:

An internist-lessee of a renovated facility found that serious errors had been made in bathroom design. Doors opened inward, and the rooms themselves were so small that, if a patient collapses on the floor, entry by another person would have been barred. Further there were no emergency bells to alert staff if a patient fell or was otherwise immobilized in the rooms.

Recommendation: Design bathrooms with the knowledge that sick and incapacitated people will be using them. If you are moving into a new facility, investigate the bathrooms with these concerns in mind. If you already have a facility with inadequate bathrooms, you should, at the very least, install emergency bells and regularly inspect and maintain the rooms. Finally, if feasible, attempt a low-cost renovation to improve the bathroom's layout.

Throughout this chapter, we have discussed ways to reduce the chance that you will be sued by concerning yourself with the physical structure of your office.

However, an equally important issue is how to discourage lawsuits by using the proper legal structure for your practice. By using professional corporations, limited liability companies, limited partnerships, and even trusts in certain situations, you can effectively discourage lawsuits before they become financially and emotionally draining.

Chapter 8: Self-Assessment Guide

Liabilities to Employees and Staff

- Do you have an employee manual that outlines all policies regarding discrimination, harassment, etc?
- Has a labor lawyer familiar with your state rules on employment, as well as federal guidelines, reviewed your policies and mandatory postings in your office?
- Liabilities Because of Staff or Employees
- Have you made clear in employment contracts, manuals, or other policy statements that you will not allow nonmedical staff to dispense medical advice? Are there repercussions if an employee fails to follow this rule?
- Have you made clear in employment contracts, manuals, or other policy statements all reports should be seen by the physicians before filing? Do you have some type of initial or check-off system?
- Have you made clear in employment contracts, manuals, or other policy statements that all patient contacts should be noted in patients' charts?

Liabilities From the Medical Office Premises

The following form can be used as a basis for inspection of your office premises.

Office Premises Checklist

- Driveway and parking lot are well-marked, with arrows, and signs. Views in the lot are unobstructed by signs and/or landscaping.

  Yes ___________ No ___________
  Comment ________________________

- Stairwell leading to entrance is in good repair, clear of debris, free of ice or is salted, and has adequate railing.

  Yes ___________ No ___________
  Comment ________________________

- Entrance is handicapped-accessible and ramp is also free of debris and ice.

  Yes ___________ No ___________
  Comment________________________

- Front door and other doors open easily and leave room for pedestrian traffic (and gurneys, if applicable).

  Yes ___________ No ___________
  Comment ________________________

- Other stairwells are in good repair, free from debris, and have adequate railing.

  Yes ___________ No ___________
  Comment ________________________

- All walkways, including hallways, are in good repair (no carpeting sticking up) and are level.

  Yes ___________ No ___________
  Comment ________________________

- All wet areas are covered by nonskid matting and are clearly denoted by signs and/or isolated by protective barriers.

  Yes ___________ No ___________
  Comment ________________________

- All biohazardous waste is stored away from patient areas or high-traffic staff areas.

  Yes ___________ No ___________
  Comment ______________________

- All waste containers used in examination rooms are secure.

  Yes ___________ No ___________
  Comment ______________________

- All electrical equipment is in proper working order.

  Yes ___________ No ___________
  Comment ______________________

- All sharps, medications, and other potentially hazardous materials are stored away from patient's access and/or locked.

  Yes ___________ No ___________
  Comment ______________________

- Office has been childproofed (ie, electric outlets are covered, childproof locks are installed on closets, signs have been installed warning adults of their responsibility of their children).

  Yes ___________ No ___________
  Comment ______________________

- Bathrooms are dry, not slippery, and are in a good state of repair (and have emergency bells, if applicable).

  Yes _____________ No __________
  Comment ______________________

Inspection performed by

____

Date of inspection __________________

Chapter Nine

Liability in the Managed Care Delivery System

The practicing physician faces a host of liability risks under a managed care delivery system. Whether you practice as part of a large provider group, an HMO, a physician provider organization (PPO), or another type of MCO, you must be aware of the lawsuit dangers you face in this new environment.

This chapter will discuss the significant liability sources found in the managed care medical marketplace: both in the physician-run groups and networks and in MCOs, in all of their various forms.

Risks When Joining a Medical Group or Network

The percentage of physicians who have joined medical groups, particularly large medical groups or networks, has increased dramatically in the last 5 years. Many of these new groups were formed in order to compete in the new medical economic marketplace: specifically, to obtain managed-care contracts. Many physicians join these groups without realizing the lawsuit risks they will incur by signing up. Before we discuss these risks, it is important to give you some legal background on the liability of partners and employees in general.

Under current laws, you can be sued and be held financially responsible for situations in which you have no personal culpability. Because of the following legal theories, you can be forced to pay, even when you had nothing to do with the incident that incurred liability.

Dangers of partners

If you are operating your medical practice as a general partnership, you have unlimited personal liability for the acts of your partners. If your partner commits malpractice, you are financially responsible. If your partner harasses a patient or employee, you are also responsible. You can even be made to pay for the acts or omissions of your partners when you had nothing at all to do with the event leading to the lawsuit.

If you are running your practice as a general partnership, you also have unlimited personal liability for the debts of the partnership. If your partnership engages in a bad contract, or cannot pay its debts, you will be forced to pay its debts out of your own pocket. For these reasons, the general partnership is the worst legal form to run a medical practice, especially when you consider the superior legal forms you should be using in your practice

Joint and Several Liability

No matter how your practice is structured, you are vulnerable to "joint and several liability." If you and your partner(s) engage in conduct that creates liability (a joint misdiagnosis or treatment or a joint wrongful termination), the lawsuit plaintiff can come after any partner for the entire judgment amount. This means, even if you were only partially at fault, you can be forced to pay the entire award. If the jury award is $1 million, you can be forced to pay $1 million, even if the jury finds you only 10% at fault. You then have the burden of suing the other more responsible parties for reimbursement.

Captain of the Ship: Vicarious Liability

Although you may not have heard of joint and several liability before, you most likely have heard of the "captain of the ship" legal theory, more formally known as "vicarious liability," under which you will be held legally and financially responsible for your employees' acts or omissions in the scope of their employment. The more employees you have in your private practice or in your department, the more vulnerable you are to lawsuits arising from their acts or omissions.

Given this legal background, let us examine the increased liability risks of joining a large medical group or network.

Increased Partner Liability

As explained, you can be held liable for the acts and omissions of your partners, even if you had nothing to do with how the liability was created. This may occur on an even grander scale in a large medical group or network because the law may imply general partnership status on such an organization, even if the physicians do not consider themselves "partners" of the network. It all depends on the conduct of the doctors, the legal and financial responsibilities among members, and how the group or network holds itself out to the public.

If a general partnership of five or eight doctor creates liability headaches, what do you think a partnership of 50 or 100 doctors will mean? At least in your small group of partners, you have screening procedures and can monitor new partners on a daily basis. How are you to protect yourself from partners who you rarely see and who practice on the other side of town?

Increased Vicarious Liability

As explained, vicarious liability creates liability risks for physicians based on the behavior of their employees. As more partners implies greater partner liability dangers, more employees implies increased vicarious liability risks.

Questions to Ask

When evaluating whether or not to join a large group or network, be sure to ask the following questions: (1) Do you really know what kinds of liability they are committing you to when they negotiate with and for you? (2) For what types of lawsuits will they cover you? (3) Where does the network's interests conflict with yours regarding liability or fighting and settling lawsuits? (4) Have you hired staff that is new to the practice and that may get you into trouble with insurance companies? (5) Have you put yourself in a situation in which you may be liable under antitrust laws? All of these are very serious considerations, but they may not have clear-cut, easy answers.

Risks When Joining a Managed-Care Organization

Joining an MCO can be beneficial for a practicing physician. We can enjoy increases in the number of patients we treat, increases in overall revenue, and a steady, reliable source of income. However, many physicians have serious complaints about practicing in a managed-care environment.

These complaints range from a loss of professional autonomy and an interference with the traditional doctor—patient relationship to an increase in demand for administrative tasks and a reduction in income. But perhaps the most alarming consequence of managed care for physicians has been the increase in potential sources of lawsuit liability. The following outlines the doctor's significant liability risks when joining an MCO such as an HMO or PPO.

Contractual Liability

Vague or Absent Provisions on Obligations and Responsibilities. Vague or absent descriptions of the various responsibilities of the MCO and the physician can create lawsuits, if the physician's behavior is interpreted by the MCO as violating a contractual provision. In fact, a physician can be liable under the contract, even when there is no negligence. Moreover, courts have used language in the MCO contract to imply a standard of care against which the physician's conduct would be judged, even if the language was not intended to create such a standard. This is exactly what happened in the recent Massachusetts case *St. Charles v Kender.*[34]

Case Study

In Kender, a physician was sued for malpractice on the basis that he allegedly failed to return several phone calls from a pregnant patient. The patient, who had a miscarriage, alleged that the failure to return her calls constituted a breach of the physician's obligations under his HMO contract. Although the physician's HMO contract made no specific mention of the duty to return phone calls promptly, it did require that the physician act "in a manner consistent with professional standards of medical care generally accepted in the medical community at the time" Moreover, the patient's MCO policy stated that, if the patient could not reach her primary-care physician within a "reasonable time" (defined as 1 to 2 hours), an administrator would be available on call to assist in obtaining health care.

Even though the trial court refused to find contractual liability against the physician, the appeals court reversed the decision. That court concluded that the physician's failure to respond for 2 days, when the plan viewed a reasonable length of response time as 1 to 2 hours, was a violation of the physician's duties to the patient.

Although the patient in this case ultimately failed to prove that a breach of the duty of care caused any injuries to her, the case is important because it shows how the law may impose a legal duty between physician and patient through the language of the MCO agreement.

Early Creation of the Doctor-Patient Relationship. It is a well-established rule in American case law that a doctor-patient relationship must be established before a patient can recover against a physician for medical malpractice. Traditionally, this relationship could only be created by a meeting between doctor and patient; however, the emergence of managed-care contracts have allowed courts to imply such a relationship when a healthcare plan's doctor is consulted before the doctor ever meets the patient face-to-face. If such a relationship is established, a malpractice action may proceed, as a duty of care to the patient will be imposed upon the physician.

According to one court's rationale, stated in a now- famous case out of Texas, a managed-care contract may actually create a doctor-patient relationship between you (as a plan physician) and every plan member the moment you sign the contract, regardless of whether or not you have met the particular patient.

Case Study

In this case, *Hand v Tavera and Humana Hospital*[35], a 49-year-old man with a history of hypertension and a father who died of an aneurysm presented at the defendant hospital emergency room complaining of hypertension, nausea, and headaches. After treating the patient with medication and after 2 to 3 hours of observation, the emergency-room physician, Dr. Boyle, decided to admit the patient with a diagnosis of "hypertension emergency." Because the patient was a member of the Humana Health Care Plan, Dr Boyle had to obtain authorization from Dr. Tavera, who was responsible for admissions that evening, Dr. Tavera disagreed with hospitalization, and although Dr. Boyle objected and so documented in his notes, Dr. Boyle could not admit the patient himself. The patient feared that he might have to pay for the admission himself, so he declined admission and returned home. A few hours later, the patient suffered a stroke that required weeks of hospitalization and that let him disabled and unable to work.

The patient eventually sued the hospital, Dr. Boyle and Dr. Tavera. The hospital according to those familiar with the case, settled for a sizable amount. Dr. Boyle was dropped because of lack of cause. Dr. Tavera moved to dismiss the case on the grounds that no doctor-patient relationship had been established, as he had neither met not talked with the patient. Although the trial court agreed with Dr. Tavera's arguments, the appellate court reversed the decision, holding that the contracts in the Humana Health Plan brought the patient and Dr. Tavera "together just as surely as though they had met directly and entered the physician-patient relationship." More important was the general rule that the court pronounced: "when a health plan's insured show up at a participating hospital emergency room, and the plan's doctor on call is consulted about the treatment or admission, there is a doctor-patient relationship between the doctor and the insured."

This principle theoretically extends the doctor-patient relationship between managed-care physicians and all plan members the moment the physician signs a contract with a MCO and, when called upon, may owe each enrollee a contractually articulated duty of care. Moreover, when performing utilization review or on- call coverage, the MCO physician may be viewed as acting within the scope of a doctor-patient relationship, even though the physician has never seen or spoken to the patient.

Violation of "Gag Rules" A common clause in many of the more recent MCO agreements is what is commonly referred to as a "gag rule." This rule essentially prohibits physicians from communicating openly with patients regarding the quality of their care, the MCO's administrative procedures, and financial incentives, among other topics. An example of such a clause is the following: "The physician agrees not to take any action or make any comment that undermines or could undermine the confidence of enrollees, potential enrollees, their employers, their unions, or the public in [name of MCO] or the quality of care which it provides."

Recommendation: Try to resist signing MCO agreements with this type of language in them. We realize, however, that often this is not viable, because of the inequity of the bargaining positions involved. Thus, if you are practicing under an MCO agreement with a "gag rule," you are in a difficult bind: Acting with a patient's best interests in mind may subject you to contractual liability.

Risk Sharing. Many of today's MCO plans now use some type of risk sharing in the form of "withhold pools" or physician—capitation arrangements. In the former, the MCO withholds part of the physician's payment until the end of the year. At that time, the physician-controlled expenses are measured against the amount budgeted toward health care for the doctor's entire patient group. If the plan is at or under budget, the "withheld pool" is given to the physician. However, if expenses exceed budgeted amounts, part or all of the pool (which can be a sizable portion of income) may be forfeited. Similarly, in a fully capitated arrangement, a substantial portion of a doctor's income can be at risk if expenses are not within budgeted parameters.

Not only do these risk-sharing arrangements put much of your income at risk, but they may create liability problems as well. The law (as you will learn later) puts the ultimate responsibility for the patient's well-being squarely on the treating physician, not the MCO. If you are seen to be considering your own financial stake when evaluating the proper choice of treatment for a patient, your liability can be enormous. Such behavior clearly constitutes a breach of your legal duty to the patient. More importantly, this is the type of conduct that inflames juries, causing them to bring back astronomical awards against both the MCO and physician.

Recommendation: Think twice if you are considering a MCO arrangement that includes some type of risk sharing. It is probably unethical and should be avoided if at all possible.

Other Contractual Issues. Your MCO agreement may contain a nonassignment that prohibits you from assigning your rights and duties under the contract, unless the MCO gives its written consent. This prohibition could have a significant impact on the market value of your practice when you choose to sell it because any other physician, group, or hospital would be barred from assuming the care of your MCO patients.

Although your MCO contract may prevent you from freely assigning your interest in the agreement, it may allow the MCO to assign its rights and duties without either notice to, or approval by, you. This language creates the risk that, in the future, you could be faced with an entirely different patient group, under new practice guidelines, utilization rules, and possibly reduced fee schedules.

Recommendation: Preferred contract language would allow you to transfer the rights and duties under the agreement in the event of your selling your practice, but in all other cases, each side would need the written consent of the other party in order to assign. This is the language for which you should negotiate.

Termination Policy. The key risks here are what are the guidelines/procedures for how the MCO might terminate you and how far in advance you must give the MCO notice that you wish to resign. Make sure you understand these rules before signing the contract.

Notification of Patient Transfer. Make sure that your MCO agreement spells out the procedure for notifying patients that their care is to be transferred to another physician and the procedure for actually transferring such care. If the policies are not clearly delineated in the contract, chances are that, in practice, the process is vague, flawed, or nonexistent. Patients who have been burned by an inadequate transfer process could bring a claim of abandonment against you, even after you have left the practice. You are ultimately responsible for your patient's care.

Insolvency Indenture Provisions. If your MCO becomes insolvent, you must continue the care of patients currently under treatment, but for how long? This eventuality should be spelled out in the contract, so there are no hidden surprises if this scenario unfolds.

Recommendation: Negotiate with the MCO before signing any agreement. Cross out problematic language, and write in alternatives. Or better yet, hire an attorney experienced in this area to negotiate for you. Remember, the MCO wants your patients and your reputation in the medical community; make them work for it. Even if your negotiations do not result in a better contract, you will be no worse off for trying.

Vicarious Liability

As explained earlier, vicarious liability means liability for the acts or omissions of another. (Earlier, this concept was introduced regarding your liability for your employees). In the managed-care context, this legal theory is important because MCOs may be held vicariously liable for the acts and omission of its plan physicians. In response to this danger, many MCOs have attempted to shift this lawsuit liability away from themselves and back to the individual physicians. This is accomplished through what is either called an "indemnification" or "hold harmless" clause (they are the same).

Many MCO contracts have one (or both) of two types of "hold harmless" clauses. The first type indemnifies the MCO against lawsuits arising out of the physician's negligence; that is, you will have to reimburse the MCO for any costs (including judgments and attorneys fees) incurred in defending or settling any claim arising from your acts or omissions. Although this clause shifts a significant lawsuit liability risk back to the physician, the more onerous type of "hold harmless" clause includes both this shift and additional risks.

The second and more dangerous type of hold "harmless clause" indemnifies the MCO against lawsuits arising out of the physician's negligence and lawsuits in which the MCO itself caused the injury. This includes cases in which an MCO's utilization review decision resulted in a delay or denial of services. The especially dangerous aspect of this type of clause stems from the fact that professional liability insurers ordinarily only cover negligent conduct of the insured physician. Therefore, this vicarious liability for the MCO's decision may not be covered under a malpractice insurance policy. The result: If you are operating under a contract with this type of clause, you can be held personally liable for the injuries the MCO causes, without any help from your liability insurance carrier.

Practice Liabilities

For Denial of Care. Although a MCO may deny a request for admission or consultation, or may insist on a premature discharge, it always remains the ultimate responsibility of the physician to do what he or she believes is necessary for proper patient care. This rule, which can subject the physician to difficult dilemmas, as well as professional liability, was clearly pronounced in a now famous California case. In short: you can be held legally and financially responsible for a MCO's denial of care if you have not appealed the denial and argued the medical necessity of the recommended test or procedure.

Case Study

The California case mentioned above was Wickline v State of California.[36] In Wickline, the patient underwent aortofemoral bypass surgery and a lumbar sympathectomy. Because of postoperative complications, her physicians requested 8 days of additional hospitalization. The Medi-Cal consultant (a general surgeon who no longer performed procedures) approved only 4 days, without consulting the surgeon who performed the procedure or the patient's record. The patient's physicians did not protest the decision. The patient returned home after 4 days and developed gangrene. She had to undergo an above-knee amputation.

In the malpractice suit that followed, filed only against Medi-Cal, not against the physicians, Medi-Cal was successful. Nonetheless, the court's pronouncements made it clear that physicians could be liable in such situations. "The physician who complies without protest with the limitations on treatment imposed by a third-party payer when the physician's medical judgment dictates otherwise, cannot avoid his ultimate responsibility for his patients' care."

This case demonstrates the legal rule that you can be held liable with situations in which the MCO ultimately makes the denial of care decision, unless you vehemently protest against the MCO's decision.

Recommendations

1. Advocate for the care warranted by your patient's condition. Make

your case to the MCO decision makers in writing. Offer a reasonable alternative to any rejected treatment plan. Move up within the MCO as necessary, in order to reach the top decision maker.

2. Level with your patients. Obtain their informed consent to, or refusal of, treatment.

For Delay of Care. Because of the liability-shifting effects of "hold harmless" clauses, and because you have the ultimate responsibility for patient's care, a delay in care resulting from the MCO's process can cause liability as well. In fact, the legal theory is identical to that described for denial of care: The doctor is ultimately responsible for the patient, even if the MCO was the party delaying the treatment or test. You can be held responsible when the MCO delay causes injury, unless you vehemently protest the delay and stay on top of the situation.

For Restriction of Services. Just as a MCO's denial or delay of care can mean lawsuit liability for you, so can the MCO's restricting of access to specialists, pharmaceuticals, treatment facilities, laboratories, and imaging centers.

For Abandonment. Let us assume that you are a consultant specialist, and the primary-care physician has approved your treatment plan for one of her patients, but does not authorize follow-up appointments. Perhaps the physician does not feel qualified to provide follow-up care. In this situation, as you have set out the treatment plan for the patient, you can be liable for abandonment if the patient does not receive follow- up treatments. Therefore, you may have a duty to provide such follow-up care yourself.

Recommendations

1. Provide appropriate care. Document any disagreements with the primary-care physician in a persuasive letter to the MCO. Ask the MCO's medical director to arbitrate the dispute.

2. Guard against unduly alarming your patient, but do not become an apologist for the MCO. Patients may be able to push the MCO along more rapidly.

Gatekeeper Liability

For physicians forced to act as gatekeepers in the managed-care environment, there is great pressure to reduce utilization of services and extend their own treatment regimens. This pressure is especially powerful if there are financial pressures to do so. MCO agreements have extended the range of primary-care treatment to include the removal of sutures, performance of all nonhospital postoperative care, perform and interpret electrocardiograms, perform flexible sigmoidoscopies, and splint and immobilize simple fracture and sprains. This pressure to increase gatekeeper responsibilities can have disastrous liability effects leading to an increase in "failure to diagnose," "failure to perform," and even negligence claims, as primary-care physicians are asked to do more with dwindling time and resources.

Also, gatekeepers may be liable for referrals to contract generated specialists. A patient may successfully recover against you for a negligent referral if you have not thoroughly checked out the physicians to whom you refer.

Recommendations

1. Ask the MCO for credentials and background on its affiliated specialists. If you cannot observe potential referrals first-hand, speak with someone who has. Call the referral specialist and ask for the names or primary care physicians who refer to them. Call these doctors, and assess the situation from their point of view.

2. Check with the MCO's medical director to see if the organization has received any complaints with unfamiliar referral physicians.

Administrative Liability

For Medical Peer Review. Peer review is an integral part of any MCO, whether it comes in the form of credentialing, quality assurance, or utilization review. Although both federal and state law provide some protection for physicians performing peer review activities, the liability exposure for doctors in this area cannot be overstated. Not only can you face adverse economic effects if you are disciplined under peer review, you can also be subject to an antitrust action (brought by a disciplined doctor) merely for participating in the review. Such actions bring stiff penalties including treble damages and prevailing attorney's fees.

For Credentialing. Physicians who take responsibility for the credentialing of new doctors and the recredentialing of participating doctors face lawsuit liability. Despite the lack of helpful guidelines to follow, you can be liable if it is judged that you did not do enough to protect patients from "foreseeable harm" in credentialing other doctors.

Recommendation: If you will participate in medical peer review or credentialing, be sure that your professional liability insurance policy covers such activity. If not, you should insist that the organization for which you are performing these services provides liability coverage for this activity.

There are numerous liability concerns for the physician practicing in the managed-care environment. Be sure to understand the risks you are engaging in when you sign an MCO agreement and begin treating MCO patients. As always, it is a wise idea to consult with experts whenever you have questions and concerns. Better to negotiate a fair deal at the outset then to agree and later try to limit your liability.

Chapter 9: Self-Assessment Checklist

1. When you joined your medical group or network, did you have counsel review their managed care organization contracts, especially on liability issues?

2. If you are in solo practice, did you have counsel review any contracts of the medical plans you accepted?

3. When a patient's treatment is initially denied by an MCO, do you act as an advocate for your patients' treatment? Do you make your case in writing and keep a copy on the file?

4. Do you work with the MCO's medical director or arbitrator when disputes are not resolved in the patient's favor?

Chapter Ten

Managing Privacy Risks: HIPAA & Beyond

Some of the most important legislation affecting how physicians practice are the new privacy protections passed by Federal and State governments in the last few years. Most well-known are the protections that were enacted under the Health Insurance Portability and Accountability Act, commonly know as "HIPAA.

According to Congress, HIPAA's purpose is "to improve portability and continuity of health insurance coverage in the group and individual markets, to combat waste, fraud, and abuse in health insurance and health care delivery, to promote the use of medical savings accounts, to improve access to long-term care services and coverage, to simplify the administration of health insurance, and for other purposes." One of these "other purposes" is certainly to protect the individual's privacy right in their confidential medical information.

Once this statute became law, and parallel state legislation was enacted, a new and important risk faced practicing physicians: the risk of violating the privacy protections now imposed on physicians and their offices.

As our goal is to give you practical knowledge and advice on how to reduce this risk in your practice, we think it is imperative that we first familiarize you with basic concepts surrounding privacy protection. Also, in this 2010 edition of the monograph, we will explain the significant impact that the 2009 Health Information Technology for Economic and Clinical Health Act ("HITECH Act") has had on HIPAA rules.

1. What "privacy" means

There are many ways to define "privacy"—it is a broad concept that includes many meanings. Here, we are really focusing on "information privacy"—the ability to control how data about the patient is collected, used and disclosed.

Even within this definition, there are various challenges. Specifically, you will need to address both information privacy policies and practices (like the kind your hospital, managed care organization or group practice has developed); and technical, physical and administrative information security practices, that protect computerized data systems.

2. Why protect privacy?

Of course, the obvious answer to this question is "because you have to." Without the legal burden, however, you might not spend the time, inconvenience and expense associated with data protection. However, you should. The duty to protect patient confidentiality goes beyond a legal duty to a professional responsibility. Consider these points:

- As we noted in the introduction, protecting patients' privacy is inherently "the right thing to do." Respect for patients means respecting their wishes about uses and disclosures of their health information.

- Privacy protection is necessary for good outcomes. Patients will not receive good care if concerns about privacy make them afraid to reveal information to health providers.

- Privacy protection is necessary for the overall public health system, too. Public health surveillance, health outcomes (cost effectiveness) studies, and health care research all depend on accurate data.

Privacy is not just a nicety; it is essential for the health system to function at all.

3. What federal law (HIPAA) requires—overview

As we explained above, HIPAA is an abbreviation for Health Insurance Portability and Accountability Act. As it applies here, HIPAA aims to improve accountability in part through what it calls administrative simplification—a term that roughly translates as "promoting efficiency."

The principal means of promoting efficiency is increased use of information technology. Compared to other parts of the economy, health care is relatively "uncomputerized"—particularly in its use of paper for health records. As HIPAA requires more use of computer systems, it also addresses worries about compromises of patient information.

Four standards, four parts

HIPAA has three health information standards and three associated regulations or "rules." These rules are as follows:

A. standardize formats for all computer-to-computer information exchanges (the "transactions standard");

B. standardize "identifiers" for health providers, health plans and patients;

C. implement information system security standards; and privacy standards.

Who is covered?

Almost every organization that provides or pays for health services, or exchanges health data of any kind, is within the reach of HIPAA. All health care providers (physicians, nurses, etc.), all health care facilities, all health plans (HMOs, insurers), and all health information clearinghouses are covered entities.

The law extends protections, or "rights", to every patient whose information is collected, used or disclosed by such covered entities. It imposes responsibilities on the workforce of a covered entity in order to secure those rights (including all employees and volunteers). The law reaches even to the business associates of health care institutions—that is, to any companies that handle health care information on a covered entity's behalf.

What is covered?

Under HIPAA, protected health information (PHI) is very broadly defined. Anything related to the "past, present or future physical or mental health condition" of a person is covered by the law's standards. Only adequately de-identified information—where it would be virtually impossible to identify the person to whom the data refers—is unprotected. While HIPAA transaction, identifier and security rules cover only electronic information, its privacy provisions apply to all paper, electronic or oral communications of PHI.

4. HIPAA Requirements in Practice

Obviously, this short chapter is not designed to replace a full-scale HIPAA compliance manual for your practice. It is designed to be a basic outline of rules and responsibilities. Your practice should be guided by an appropriate HIPAA practice consultant.

Notification of rights

HIPAA requires covered entities—including the physician practices—to provide patients with a notice of privacy practices. The Notice must describe, in general terms, how organizations will protect health information, and specify the patient's right to:

1. gain access to and, if desired, obtain a copy of his/ her own health records;
2. request corrections of errors that the patient finds (or to include a statement of disagreement about errors the institution refuses to change);
3. receive an accounting of how their information has been used (including a list of the persons and institutions to whom/which it has been disclosed);
4. request limits on access to, and additional protections for, particularly sensitive information;
5. request confidential communications (by alternative means or at alternative locations) of particularly sensitive information;
6. complain to the facility's privacy officer if there are problems; and
7. pursue the complaint with the US Department of Health and Human Services' Office of Civil Rights if the problems are not satisfactorily resolved.

A copy of the Notice must be provided the first time a patient sees a direct treatment provider, and any time thereafter when requested. Health plans and insurers must also provide periodic Notices.

Acknowledgments and Authorizations

On that first visit, treatment providers must also make a "good faith effort" to obtain a written acknowledgment, confirming that a copy of the Notice was obtained. This is the moment when providers should discuss patients' particular privacy questions and concerns.

In emergency situations, the acknowledgment process can be deferred. (Note that the acknowledgment does not affirm that the patient understands what is in the

Notice, just receipt of it.) The requirement for a signed acknowledgment replaces the consent requirement in an earlier version of the Privacy Rule. Covered entities may still ask the patient to sign a consent form, but the practice is not entirely optional under HIPAA.

No additional documentation is required from the patient to use or disclose information for basic functions, like treatment and payment, or for a broad range of other core health care operations. However, patients must sign a supplemental authorization before information can be used for "extra" purposes like research, or certain kinds of marketing and fundraising.

Health care institutions cannot condition treatment or payment for health care services on receiving a patient's authorization for such supplemental uses.

Four information categories covered

The general rule under HIPAA is a simple one: if a person has a right to make a health care decision, then he/she has the right to control information associated with that decision.

Children and those who are incompetent may have decisions about both health care and health information made by a personal representative. (Typically, the personal representative is the parent in the case of a child.).

One way to think about use and disclosure of protected health information under HIPAA is by putting it into four categories:

1. covered by an acknowledgment of Notice (and perhaps an optional consent), which includes routine treatment, payment and other health care operations;
2. requiring a supplemental authorization, such as research, marketing or fundraising;
3. requiring an opportunity to agree or object to a practice, but no consent or authorization; and
4. not requiring even an opportunity to agree or object.

We have already discussed the first two. The third of these categories includes uses for facility directories, and disclosures to those involved in a person's care.

The fourth category includes PHI uses where there is no opportunity for the patient to agree or object to the use of the information. This occurs in certain circumstances, such as:

1. for public health activities;
2. for victims of abuse, neglect or domestic violence;
3. for health oversight activities;
4. for judicial or administrative proceedings;
5. for law enforcement;
6. about deceased persons (including organ and tissue donations);
7. where permitted by an IRB or Privacy Board waiver, for research;
8. to avert a serious, imminent threat to public safety;
9. certain specialized government functions (e.g., national security, military, corrections); or
10. anything else required by law.

Individuals would be entitled to an accounting of such disclosures, though that accounting might be temporarily suspended in certain circumstances.

Minimum necessary standard

Beyond all the above categories, HIPAA imposes a "minimum necessary standard" on persons who deal with health information: *collection, use and disclosure should be no greater than necessary to complete a work-related task.*

The minimum necessary standard does not apply to health practitioners engaged in treatment. The regulations try to avoid interfering in the daily practice of delivering health care. (That said, you, as a physician, are under a moral and professional requirement to limit information exchange to what is needed for good treatment.)

Health care facilities are under an obligation to integrate a minimum necessary into their policies and procedures for everyone other than treatment providers. That includes administrative rules as well as, where available, computer-enforced access controls. HIPAA extends extra protections for especially sensitive information, notably psychotherapy notes, which require a supplemental authorization for release.

Institutional policies and procedures

To be sure, it is a long list of standards and categories, and not one you should attempt to memorize. It is sufficient to have a sense of the overall structure. (For a more intensive exposure to the requirements, consult with an experienced HIPAA advisor).

You do need to know that every health care facility must put in place privacy policies that reflect HIPAA's requirements, and, if they are stricter, the requirements of state law. Those policies must include sanctions for employees that violate them, including termination for serious or repeated violations.

Institutions must designate a privacy officer, who will have the responsibility for enforcing the rules, as well as supervising (or handling directly) the procedures to handle requests for information access, corrections to records, accountings of disclosures, processing complaints and so forth.

Institutions must also include privacy requirements in their contracts with business associates.

Finally, all employees (and volunteers) must be educated about privacy practices in a manner "appropriate" to their job responsibilities.

Many of HIPAA's "new" protections are actually "old" ones that already are a part of your state's laws or required by norms of professional practice. Unfortunately, those rules and norms often were ignored and HIPAA was enacted on the Federal level to fill the void.

Sanctions for violations

The most important sanction for a physician is not written in any law book—it is the loss of business if patients lose confidence in its information practices. In the competitive market that has come with managed care, few health care practices can afford to lose patients, for any reason. Further, no practice can afford to keep a worker who fails to observe the privacy rules, given the substantial consequences for violations.

Beyond this business reason, HIPAA includes substantial civil and criminal penalties to encourage compliance. These penalties range from $100 per violation up to $250,000 and 10 years in prison. The harshest penalties attend deliberate misuse, particularly for sale or use of information for personal gain, commercial advantage or malicious harm. Persons convicted for such activities can expect to visit a federal prison. State penalties may also apply, along with possible disciplinary actions by certification bodies (e.g., loss of license to practice).

Failures that result from accidental disclosures are unlikely to be fined, much less result in jail time, provided reasonable steps are taken to fix the violation as soon as possible.

5. HIPAA and state law

As noted above, states have laws that also address information protection. Some have broad privacy laws, including privacy provisions in the state constitution. Almost all have laws that cover health information specifically.

In many cases, the requirements of state law are even stricter than the new federal requirements. While HIPAA adds its protections to state law, any state laws that are more protective of health privacy remain in force.

Be sure to meet with a HIPAA consultant or healthcare attorney in your state to see what your state requires in this area.

6. Civil Liability

The HIPAA regulations themselves do not grant a private right of enforcement to patients who believe themselves injured by a presumed violation of HIPAA. This means that an attorney representing a patient cannot merely file suit, alleging a violation of HIPAA. But this also does not mean there will not be an increase in privacy and confidentiality violation lawsuits. In fact, many prominent personal injury attorneys have already announced they expect this will become a large part of their practice. They will attempt to use the HIPAA regulations as standard of care when they file state approved lawsuits under privacy laws. A recent Wisconsin case illustrates this possibility.

Case Study: Helpful Disclosure Still Liable

The defendant EMT and three other members of the volunteer fire department responded to an emergency 911 call at the plaintiff's residence regarding an overdose or possible overdose. After treating the patient and transporting her to the hospital, the EMT went home and later spoke to a friend about the incident. The EMT did not know the patient personally, but knew a friend of hers and, in hoping the friend could help the patient, relayed the story. The friend then visited the plaintiff's home where she revealed some of the new information to the plaintiff's family and then to hospital personnel.

The plaintiff successfully sued the EMT, and volunteer fire department for violation of privacy—a suit that was upheld on appeal.

This case illustrates how even in very small cases, state law can be a powerful weapon when it comes to invasion of privacy and possible defamation (see below more on state law). "Good intentions" were not a successful defense, and not having a written policy in this area could also subject you to HIPAA violations, even if the lawsuit was brought under state law. HIPAA is the first law to bring a standard of patient privacy protection to all 50 states. The publicity surrounding HIPAA, and the need to inform all patients, means that public expectations and awareness are now raised among patients and attorneys.

7. What your institution requires

Beyond HIPAA and even state law, the healthcare institutions with which you are affiliated may have even more onerous requirements. Be sure to work with these institutions' privacy officers to ensure that your office is complying with their procedures as well.

8. You are also a patient

Physicians have health care needs too, of course—we see our own health care providers from time to time. Another important reason to be more familiar with HIPAA is to understand the privacy protections for our own health information. Your day-to-day behavior determines the privacy of others' health information. And, somewhere out there, the actions of other health care workers will determine how much privacy you have.

Recommendations

1. Generate an appropriate Privacy Notice and, on a patient's first visit, obtain a written acknowledgment, confirming that a copy of the Notice was obtained. This is the moment when providers should discuss patients' particular privacy questions and concerns.

2. Consult with a medical practice consultant and/or healthcare attorney to implement procedures and policies for your office to comply with HIPAA and state law requirements.

3. Speak with the privacy officers of each healthcare institution with which you are affiliated. Make the appropriate changes to your office to be in compliance with their privacy procedures.

The HITECH Act's Recent Impact on HIPAA Rules

The passage of the HITECH act—part of the American Recovery and Reinvestment Act of 2009—marked a new phase of HIPAA regulation. The sweeping changes under the HITECH Act closed many of the gaps that complicated enforcement and added regulations that increased accountability and penalties for violations. These were changes that many in the healthcare industry applauded—as giving regulations the clarity and teeth necessary to enable progress in the push for better privacy and security.

Here, we will address very briefly Subtitle D of HITECH amending the privacy and security rules under HIPAA. HIPAA's privacy and security rules established floors of confidentiality and security protections for patients' demographic and health information in all forms—paper, oral, and electronic. The development of health information technology (for example, electronic health records, personal health records, health information exchanges) up until 2009 had ` resulted in additional risks; HITECH was intended to build on the privacy and security rules to address these new risks.

Specifically, the HITECH act impacted HIPAA in a number of significant ways. The two most important, in the authors' views are the following:

1. Expanded HIPAA's reach to "business associates."

Under the privacy rule, a business associate is a person who provides a function on behalf of a covered entity (other than as part of the covered entity's workforce) that involves the use of protected health information (PHI). Examples of this type of business associate include billing services, transcription services, and answering services. A business associate is also a person who provides specified services involving the use of PHI to a covered entity. The specified services are legal, actuarial, accounting, consulting, data aggregation, management, administrative, accreditation, and financial services.

Business associates may use and disclose PHI, but only in compliance with the business associate agreement evidencing the business associate's promise to maintain the confidentiality and security of PHI. Under existing law, business associates only have contractual liability with the covered entity via the business associate agreement. As of February 2010, business associates must comply with the security rule and will be subject to government enforcement.[37]

This is obviously a massive expansion of the reach of HIPAA, to nearly any type of related service to a health provider in the normal course of business.

2. Increased HIPAA enforcement

The HITECH act also increased enforcement of HIPAA by the federal and state government. These changes include the following:

- State attorneys general can bring enforcement action for violations of federal HIPAA regulations.
- Employees and individuals are subject to HIPAA's criminal penalties.
- The Department of Health and Human Services (HHS) must conduct audits of covered entities and business associates.
- HHS must investigate complaints of willful neglect, and if substantiated, HHS must impose a statutory penalty of at least $10,000 to $50,000 per violation.
- HHS and state attorneys general can pursue civil HIPAA violations in cases in which criminal penalty could attach, but the Department of Justice declines to pursue.
- Individuals can recover a percentage of penalties imposed or settlement proceeds from HIPAA investigations based on their complaints.[38]

As you will see in the next chapter, the HITECH changes above, along with a more aggressive Department of Justice, has resulted in a new wave of criminal actions against violators of HIPAA.

Conclusion

Protecting a patient's confidential information has always been a crucial part of the physician-patient relationship. Now that duty has expanded under HIPAA, state law, and healthcare institutions' policies. As a caring physician, you want your patients to have a comfort level that their personal information will be properly protected. Only then, will they feel comfortable in providing you all the information you need to give them proper patient care. Further, only then can you be sure that you will not be liable for breaches of this confidential relationship.

Chapter 10: Self-Assessment Checklist

1. On a new patient's initial visit, do you provide them with a Privacy Notice and obtain a written acknowledgment, confirming that a copy of the Notice was obtained?

2. Has this Notice been reviewed by an outside consultant or attorney to be sure it complies with the latest Federal and State guidelines? Has it been approved by your affiliated healthcare institutions?

3. Do you understand what HIPAA's Privacy Rule requires? There are comprehensive educational resources available on the HHS Web site, <www.hhs.gov/ocr/privacy>.

4. Do you know what the Security Rule requires to protect against reasonably anticipated improper use or disclosure of electronic PHI? The Security Rule consists of 18 safeguards (administrative, physical, and technical), and for each of the three types of safeguards, there are standards (what must be done) and implementation specifications (how it must be done).

5. Most importantly, have you employed a medical practice consultant and/or healthcare attorney to implement procedures and policies for your office to comply with HIPAA, state law requirements, HITECH and those of your affiliated healthcare institutions?

Chapter Eleven

From Congress to Court: Results & Lessons from Recent HIPAA Litigation

In the prior chapter, we laid out the basic scope of the HIPAA rules, what the legislation essentially dictates, and how medical professionals can best adhere to it. In this chapter, we summarize where HIPAA has come in last 7 years, as it has become part of our healthcare system. First, we will provide some statistics in terms of claims made under the privacy provisions. Then, we will examine some of the leading legal cases that have tried to interpret what the HIPAA rules really mean.

Statistics: Few Privacy Complaints Brought under HIPAA Have Merit

According to a 2006 report by the Health Information Privacy/Security Alert, less than a quarter of the total medical privacy complaints lodged with the Department of Health and Human Services were eligible for further federal investigation of healthcare organizations covered by HIPAA. Further, the following statistics came from the same report.[39]

> Of the 22,664 complaints received by the HHS Office for Civil Rights (OCR) from April 2003, when the complaint system was started, through Sept. 30, 2006, approximately 5,400 (23.8%) merited further investigation or action, according to agency statistics.
>
> Of the 5,400 complaints that were pursued, OCR took informal action in 3,700 cases, resolving about 68%.
>
> Of the remaining 1,700 (32%), OCR found that the covered healthcare organization had not violated the privacy rule.

This means that 17,175 complaints did not meet the criteria for further investigation.

Most often, a complaint would not be eligible for investigation because the allegations in the complaint do not constitute violations of the HIPAA rules.

The top targets of OCR complaints were:

- Private healthcare practices;
- General hospitals;
- Outpatient facilities;
- Group health plans and
- Health insurance insurers; and
- Pharmacies.

The top five complaints received by OCR were:

- The impermissible use or disclosure of an individual's identifiable health information;
- The lack of adequate safeguards to protect identifiable health information;
- Refusal or failure to provide the individual with access to or a copy of his or her records;
- Disclosure of more data than is minimally necessary to satisfy a request for information; and
- Failure to have the individual's valid authorization for a disclosure that requires one.

Lessons to be Learned from the Study

What can the practicing physician learn from these statistics? A number of important lessons emerge:

1. The risk of having a patient complaint is a real one—as private healthcare practices continue to be among the most-often subjects of a complaint.
2. Merit-less complains are problematic here as they are in medical

malpractice litigation in general— as evidenced here by the high number of complaints that do not warrant investigations.

3. This is an emerging area of regulation where further study and experience is needed.

Court Rulings on HIPAA in the last decade

As with any new major legislation, once Congress has passed the law, the administrative agencies attempt to implement the law—implementing various regulations and procedures. While there is typically a few years lag time, eventually the court system will become involved, as parties either sue to have elements of the law overturned or interpreted, or be compensated for some violation thereof. In this case, there is more than the federal HIPAA rules at issue, as each state has enacted privacy legislation as well. As you will see below, these rules also need state court interpretation as well.

In the 3 years since our last publication of this monograph, we have had just enough time to see new case law made in the interpretation of HIPAA and state privacy legislation. We will summarize a few of the top cases and provide the legal citations here for your research as well.

Gunn v. Sound Shore Medical Center of Westchester, 772 N.Y.S.2d 714

In this New York case, the plaintiff was allegedly injured by a treadmill at a cardiac rehabilitation facility, which was owned by the defendant hospital. The plaintiff sought the names and addresses of the other patients who were at the facility at the time of the incident. The trial court agreed with the plaintiff, ordering the defendant hospital to disclose the patients' names. When the hospital appealed, the appellate court reversed the trial court's decision, stating "since disclosure of the patients' names will, in effect, reveal that they were undergoing treatment for cardiac-related conditions, such discovery is prohibited under [New York's physician-patient privilege law]."

The most interesting part of this case is that court referred to HIPAA even though the statute was not an issue in the case. The court said "the passage of HIPAA lends support to the conclusion that disclosure of the identity of the other patients at the center would breach the physician-patient privilege and thus should not be permitted."

This case is important as it shows how courts will use HIPAA to potentially expand the privacy protections (and liability for violations thereof) outside of the HIPAA's jurisdiction. See the cases below for similar results.

Hutton v. City of Martinez, 219 F.R.D. 164 (Northern District of California, 2003)
In this personal injury case, the defendant was a police officer who shot the plaintiff in the back. The plaintiff claimed he was shot because the defendant was physically unable to pursue the plaintiff on foot. To bolster his argument, the plaintiff sought to obtain evidence of the defendant's physical condition from the defendant's workers' compensation carrier. The workers' compensation carrier, even though explicitly excluded from the definition of a "covered entity" under HIPAA, nonetheless relied on HIPAA to refuse to produce the records related to the defendant's work- related back injury. The court found the medical records to be directly relevant and held that "HIPAA does not preclude production of the medical records and workers' compensation files in response to either a discovery request, subpoena, or this court's order, under an adequate protective order."

This was interesting because the attempted use of HIPAA by the worker's compensation carrier to shielded it from having to turn over information based on privacy grounds. Although the court did not "buy" the argument in this case, it does demonstrate the potential leveraging of HIPAA rules by parties not explicitly covered by the statute.

Acara v. Banks, 470 F.3d 569, 571 (5th Cir. 2006)
This case is significant for 2 reasons: (1) because it is the only HIPAA case that has risen to the federal circuit court level—one level below the Supreme Court—and (2) because it clearly stated that there is no private cause of action (right to sue) under the HIPAA statute. The court said specifically: "HIPAA does not contain any express language conferring private rights upon a specific class of individuals. Instead, it focuses on regulating persons that have access to individually identifiable medical information and who conduct certain electronic health transactions. Because HIPAA specifically delegates enforcement, there is a strong indication that Congress intended to preclude private enforcement."

Based on her assumption that HIPAA allowed her a private cause of action for damages, plaintiff Margaret Acara filed a claim in Louisiana Federal Court against her physician for allegedly disclosing Acara's private medical information without her consent during a deposition. However, the trial court dismissed Acara's claims on the grounds that it did not have jurisdiction over the dispute since there was no private right of action under HIPAA. The Fifth Circuit agreed and affirmed the trial court's ruling.

Acosta v. Byrum 638 S.E.2d 246 (N.C. Ct. App. 2006)

In this case,a patient sued a psychiatrist for negligent infliction of emotional distress. The basis of the patient's claims was that the defendant psychiatrist allegedly allowed his office manager access to plaintiff's mental health records.

At trial the court found that the plaintiff's claim did not specify what HIPAA standard the psychiatrist violated, and therefore granted summary judgment to the psychiatrist. The appeals court differed, stating that there was no need to specify what standard was violated, since the pleading need only put the psychiatrist on notice as to the basis of the claim. Thus, it fund that summary judgment should not have been granted.

The appeals court also noted the plaintiff's the claim here was not a HIPAA breach *per se,* but a common-law tort of negligent infliction of emotional distress. The plaintiff was simply using the HIPAA breach as evidence that the standard of care was not met.

Again, like the Gunn case above, the court here recognized that HIPAA may have implications beyond its specific jurisdiction. Here, the court found that a breach of HIPAA could be evidence of failure to meet the standard of care and, thus, liability to a patient in a private suit outside of HIPAA. This is an important development.

Examples of Criminal Indictments under HIPAA

In a recent action, an indictment by a grand jury under the U.S. attorney for the Eastern District of Arkansas may have signaled an aggressive change in direction regarding federal prosecution of HIPAA violators. In that case, a nurse pleaded guilty to a single count of a HIPAA violation. Andrea Smith, who was employed at the Northeast Arkansas Clinic in Jonesboro, Arkansas, accessed the private information of a clinic patient on Nov. 28, 2006, according to a news release. She gave the information to her husband who allegedly called the patient and threatened to use the information against the patient in an upcoming legal proceeding, the release said. With her guilty plea, charges against her husband and another charge against Smith were dropped, the release said.

Jane Duke, the U.S. attorney who brought the charge, said in the release that the Justice Department is serious about enforcing the criminal HIPAA statute, even when it comes to charging individuals. "What every HIPAA-covered entity needs to realize and reinforce to its employees is that the privacy provisions of HIPAA are serious and have significant consequences if they are violated," In the release, Duke noted that criminal enforcement of HIPAA "is a fairly new concept."[40]

Even more recently (2009), the same U.S. attorney (Jane Duke) lead an investigation where a physician and two former employees at St. Vincent Infirmary Medical Center in Little Rock, Arkansas, pleaded guilty to misdemeanor federal charges that they inappropriately accessed the medical records of local television anchor who was killed back in 2008. Both physician and employees admitted to accessing the local celebrity's medical records for purely personal interest. Specifically, the physician admitted that after watching a news report regarding Ms. Pressly being slain and taken to St. Vincent's, where he was on-staff, he logged on from home and accessed the hospital's records system to "determine if the news reports were accurate." One of the other charged employees, a former account representative at the hospital, admitted that she accessed Ms. Pressly's file about 12 times "out of curiosity." The third employee charged, an emergency room secretary, admitted that she "became curious about the patient's [Ms. Pressly's] status and accessed the medical chart to find out if the patient was still living."[41]

Conclusion on Cases

In the relatively short time that HIPAA has been law, we see a number of divergent trends developing. On one hand, the vast majority of claims brought under the law have been judged to be merit-less by the agency tasked with enforcing the law and, the highest courts of the land have confirmed that HIPAA does not afford a cause of action for a private lawsuit. On the other hand, courts have begun to use the HIPAA standards not only in actions brought strictly under its rules, but have expanded HIPAA's potential reach by utilizing its rules as general standard of care in general tort/non-HIPAA related actions. Further, the justice department has begun to pursue criminal convictions or guilty pleas under the HIPAA statute itself.

Chapter 11: Self-Assessment Checklist

1. Read the excellent list of HIPAA-related questions and answers on the American Medical Association's website at http://www.ama-assn.org/ama/pub/physician-resources/solutions-managing- your-practice/coding-billing-insurance/ hipaahealth-insurance-portability-accountability- act/ frequently-asked-questions.shtml

2. Work with a consultant or attorney experienced in HIPAA to review your practice's consent forms, procedures, and processes—to make sure they are compliant with this new and constantly-emerging area.

Chapter Twelve

Risk Management in Telemedicine

One of the fastest-growing developments in medicine since the last publication of this monograph has been in the field of telemedicine. This should not come as a surprise, given the increasing reliance on technology— especially the Internet and wireless communication— in virtually every other field of endeavor. While the advances in telemedicine may be beneficial for patient and physician alike, they also create new risks that need to be better understood and properly managed.

What is Telemedicine?

Before we examine the risks created by emerging "telemedicine," we need to define this term. The American Medical Association has defined telemedicine as "medical practice across distance via telecommunications and interactive video technology." While a layperson might ask what types of medicine can actually be practiced "virtually" under the AMA's definition, physicians understand better.

With its focus on diagnostics, where physicians read studies that can be transported easily via Internet or even wireless technology, radiology is the field in which telemedicine has grown most significantly.

Example: Tele-Radiology

Sending radiology information from one point to another (i.e. from the hospital to the radiologist's home, from one medical facility to another, etc.) has been practiced for fifteen years. A system that moves radiology images and stores them is known as a PACS system (Picture Archiving and Communication), and the system that handles the patient demographic, clinical and financial information is known as RIS (Radiology Information System). In the last seven years, a large industry has been created using RIS/ PACS technology to deliver hospital emergency scans to radiologists in the US and overseas to cover hospitals throughout the night.

Case Study: Tele-Radiology

On a cold and misty night in November, "Joan" a retired secretary, was walking across a dark parking lot outside a restaurant in which she had just eaten. She suddenly slipped and fell heavily on her right arm and shoulder. Experiencing severe pain in the arm, she suspected she might be hurt and she hailed a cab to a local hospital emergency room. The triage nurse examined Joan very briefly, took a quick history, and told her to wait to be seen by the doctor.

Three hours later Joan was finally seen by Dr Andrews, the emergency room physician. Her elbow and upper arm were bruised, there was swelling around the elbow and she had a great difficulty in rotating her forearm. Her shoulder and hip were hurting, and there was some bruising over her hip. The physician ordered x-rays of her shoulder, hip and elbow, and Joan was brought to radiology about 12:30 AM to have all studies performed.

Joan did not realize that her x-rays were not going to be read by a radiologist in the hospital, but rather they were being transmitted overseas by the Internet. The hospital had recently contracted with an overseas reading service that covered the hospital's radiology reading each night from 11PM to 7AM. This service utilized American trained radiologists who were licensed in several states. This hospital contract was a new one for this service, and the first one in Joan's state. Through a scheduling oversight, the radiologist reading Joan's films was licensed in the US, but not in the state in which the hospital was located.

Within 45 minutes, the radiologist reported Joan's case back to the ER. He reported seeing no fracture, but did comment that the films were of limited technical quality, and that repeat films and additional views should be obtained depending on the patient's clinical presentation. The busy ER physician obtained the negative report from the secretary who received the faxed report. He did not order any additional films, and discharged Joan home with ice packs and instructions to see her internist the next day.

At 9AM the following morning, Dr. Smith, one of the hospital radiologists, reviewed Joan's films. He found that the three fractures around the elbow that he recognized has not been reported by the teleradiology service. He immediately called the ER, and spoke with the attending physician for the day, as Dr. Andrews had gone off shift and was no longer in the hospital. Dr. Smith transmitted his concern that with the fractures and dislocation he saw, the patient could suffer nerve damage if untreated.

The ER physician put in place the hospital's call back policy for its ER patients, and within twenty minutes Joan was being told that she must return to the hospital for further treatment. This time there was no delay when she entered the emergency room. An orthopedic surgeon met her shortly after she arrived and his assessment confirmed the fears of the radiologist that Joan had suffered nerve impairment. He took her to the OR, reduced the fractures and dislocation, but the nerve damage remained. Joan would never again regain total use of that arm.

Within a day, the Director of risk management at the hospital had been notified and was investigating this case. What she found out did not please her. After notifying the hospital malpractice insurer, she discovered that her state required that any institution using out of hospital facilities to provide care was obligated to notify its patients of that policy. Not only was the risk management director unaware of this policy, she discovered that the rest of the staff were also uninformed. She realized that doctors providing care to hospital patients must be licensed in her state, but not until later did she discover that this was not true in Joan's case. Finally, to her dismay, she found out that the hospital had not even followed its own policy of credentialing physicians when it came to contracting with the nightcall radiology provider. None of the tele-radiology physicians were even listed on the hospital staff.

The Director then did a more thorough investigation of the tele-radiology contract. She found there were no requirements for HIPAA certification in the contract, and that quality issues regarding film resolution were not addressed. There wasn't even a clear hospital privacy policy included in the contract. When she asked for a copy of the insurance policy covering this contract, she discovered that the limits of liability the hospital required were present, but that there were aggregate limits applying to all 22 of the radiologists reading for this group, not for any one radiologist. Furthermore, she found out that two other cases were pending against the group, and that by the time they got to her case, the insurance limits might be met.

This case illustrates many of the potential problems associated with telemedicine practice, and it is a very possible scenario in any facility. While the results in this case were severe for Joan, many cases occur daily with minimal negative results but with the same risk factors present.

What Are the Key Risk Management Issues Specific to Telemedicine?

Telemedicine practice complicates issues of risk management for several reasons. Let's briefly review them here. For the following discussion, the authors wish to acknowledge the extremely helpful article of healthcare attorneys Tara Kepler and Charlene L. McGinty.[42]:

1. First, the traditional physician-patient relationship with face-to-face consultations is now potentially complicated by communication technology. By potentially adding emotional as well as physical distance between physician and patient, technology may actually alter that essential relationship. Kepler and McGuinty expand on this idea, recognizing that the boundaries of the physician-patient relationship created by these virtual encounters are not yet well-established in case law, as of their 2009 article.

However, the attorneys note that courts have reviewed other indirect encounters and have developed applicable guidelines for determining whether a physician-patient relationship has been formed pursuant to a remote telemedicine encounter. These courts have used the following types of guidelines for determining if a physician-patient relationship existed:

- A physician-patient relationship may exist even though the physician and patient have never had direct contact;
- A physician-patient relationship may exist where others have contracted with the physician on the patient's behalf;
- A physician-patient relationship exists if the relationship was contracted for or with the express or implied consent of the patient or for the patient's benefit; and
- A physician-patient relationship exists when health care services are rendered on behalf of the patient and are done for the patient's benefit.[43]

2. Secondly, since the professional relationship with patients through telemedicine has not been well defined, the courts and medical boards will need to make such definitions in the near future. They are also likely to use traditional perspectives to more clearly define whether a professional relationship exists in each of the variety of new circumstances created by technology, e.g., email, chat rooms, videoconferencing using Internet or ISDN lines.

3. Third, as we stated in the 2007 edition of this text, "the respective roles and potential liability of referring physicians and consulting physicians is even more ambiguous. The definition of negligence with respect to either or both types of physician is unclear. These roles and definitions are likely to undergo a similar process of re-definition as the direct physician-patient relationship above."

Kepler and McGuinty pick up on this, discussing the standard of care that might be applied to a situation where a telemedicine physician had created a duty of care to a patient based on the doctor-patient relationship. They explain that some courts prefer using a local or community standard of care, while others use a national standard of care."If a community standard is used, multi-state telemedicine encounters complicate the analysis. Which community should the court use as the reference point—the patient's or the physician's? It would be onerous to assume that the physician should be knowledgeable of multiple community standards of care. Alternatively, using the standard of care in the patient's community would also be reasonable because standards of medical care are primarily regulated by states to protect the patients located within the state. State regulation of medicine is rarely a tool for accommodating to the professional preferences of physicians located in the state… For example, some states have created telemedicine-specific informed consents standards, privacy standards and general telemedicine standards of care, as discussed above. This creates an additional, heightened standard of care to which the physician's actions might be compared in a telemedicine negligence or malpractice."[44]

Does this mean that a national standard of care should be adopted? It might make things easier in this context, but it may have significant unwanted effects on telemedicine as whole.

4. Fourth, jurisdictional issues emerge when telemedicine is practiced over state—and even country-lines. As it stands, telemedicine physicians could be subject to the jurisdiction of the state where they reside, every state where they practice, and the state where the patient resides. The respective liabilities of institutions housing such services are also ambiguous.

Kepler and McGuinty state emphatically that "the inability to predict how courts will allocate loss related to a given telemedicine encounter is a formidable barrier to multi-state telemedicine programs." However, they recommend physicians and risk managers begin by identifying the following:

- The possible states into which the telemedicine program and physicians are reaching; and
- The similarities and differences in medical malpractice law for the identified states.

In an attempt to address some of the legal ambiguities of telemedicine encounters, the attorneys explain, some states have crafted telemedicine-specific statutes that affect medical malpractice analyses. Some states have statutorily defined the location of the telemedicine act as the physical location of the patient. Some states have even subjected out-of-state physicians to the laws of their state if the physician practices medicine in their state through telemedicine or utilize a licensure exception to provide temporary or consultative services to in-state patients.[45]

Getting Advice is Critical

This area, like HIPAA, is changing rapidly, due to constantly emerging state and federal legislation, new cases in the courts, and medical self-regulatory standards. Further, given the comments above and the references to the leading article by the healthcare attorneys referenced above, this is a complex area of risk management. Therefore, it is critical, that if you want advice in this area, you consult a healthcare attorney, risk management consultant, or other local professional who works in this area.

Nevertheless, we have attempted to pick out common advice from our research. Please see the checklist below for this "common sense" advice—much of it coming from a particular well-respected consultant.[46]

Chapter 12: Self-Assessment Checklist

1. Read and understand your state laws regarding telemedicine liability. Consult with an attorney if you need help here. Subscribe to publications to keep yourself current on these and other laws passed in your state.

2. Weigh the advantages and disadvantages to becoming licensed and credentialed in all states for which you intend to provide telemedicine services. Some states have specific "telemedicine licenses" but most require full licensure in that state to practice at all, regardless of the method.

3. Obtain professional liability insurance coverage for the specific duties you are performing in telemedicine; understand the limits of your liability for

telemedicine practice, and obtain the details of coverage as well as limits of your liability for telemedicine practice from your specific carrier. Obtain a written agreement from your carrier regarding their coverage of your specific program and its specific services. Do not settle for written agreements or "form" letters that don't specify your program and its services.

4. Provide patients with written lists of alternatives and behavioral suggestions in the case of equipment failure, accident or catastrophe. Have a backup plan that includes referrals to local practitioners in your specialty if necessary, should the Internet or other communication system you rely on fail for any reason.

5. When delivering innovative service in an area where validated research has not yet been established, fully inform all clients both verbally and in writing of such practice as: being outside the standard, and in an area not yet validated by research. In the consent form, include issues such as advantages and limitations of telemedicine service delivery, including inherent deficiencies in the electronic equipment possibly interfering with diagnosis or treatment; issues related to equipment failure; choice of venue waivers to resolve issues of jurisdiction; a brief description of equipment and services to be delivered, the purpose, benefits, potential risks and other consequences of services delivered. Describe the specific roles of the consultant and local referring practitioner; which one has ultimate authority over the patient's treatment, and that the information will be stored in a computerized data base.

6. Be sure to inform patients of practitioner licensure, and provide state licensing board contact information. Collect patient satisfaction measures regularly throughout service delivery. Arrange for proper scanning and sharing of release forms signed by patients so that local practitioner, remote consultants and patients themselves can have copies for their files.

7. Be certain that your staff is following whatever standards of care might exist in telemedicine for your program specialty area. Check with your professional associations for their statements regarding telemedicine practice, research, or education. This may include technical requirements of the sending and viewing technology as in specialties of radiology, cardiology, dermatology, pathology.

8. Seek vendors willing and able to provide:

    - support 24/7 to train new staff and patients, as well as avoid errors leading to data destruction.
    - downtime instructions for accessing emergency information during scheduled and unscheduled downtimes.
    - contracts that detail specific protections and maintenance services to be implemented.
    - clear documentation for regular maintenance requirements, procedures, and logs to record such maintenance.
    - backup systems, such as an alternate equipment, power sources and off-line data storage.
    - documentation of disaster recovery protocols.

References

1. "National Jury-Award Median in Medical Malpractice Cases"; Jury Verdict Research®, Horsham, PA.

2. Perlman, Peter, "Don't Punish the Injured," *American Bar Association Journal* (May 1986).

3. *NAIC Profitability by Line by State, 2001, presented before the House Judiciary Committee by the Physicians' Insurance Association of America (PIAA), June 2002.*

4. Kessler, Daniel, "Impact of Malpractice Reforms on the Supply of Physicians," *Journal of the American Medical Association (JAMA) June 1, 2005—Vol 293, No. 21.*

5. Weinstein, Dr. Stuart L., "The Cost of Defensive Medicine," *AAOS Now* (November 2008).

6. National Practitioner Data Bank, 2006 Annual Report, U.S Department of Health & Human Services, p 26.

7. Physicians Insurers Association of America. *Claims Trend Analysis: 2009 Edition.* Rockville, MD, 2009.

8. Physicians Insurers Association of America. *Claims Trend Analysis: 2009 Edition.* Rockville, MD, 2009

9. Ostergard N, Volk L. "Overview of CRICO claims data." *Forum.* 1996; 17(.3):2-6.

10. Physicians Insurers Association of America. Breast Cancer Study. Rockville, Md: June 1995.

11. Physicians Insurers Association of America. Breast Cancer Study. Rockville, Md: March 1990.

12 Physicians Insurers Association of America. Breast Cancer Study: 3rd Edition. Rockville, Md: 2002.

13. Physicians Insurers Association of America. Breast Cancer Study: 3rd Edition. Rockville, Md: 2002.

14. Physicians Insurers Association of America. Breast Cancer Study. Rockville, Md: March 1990.

15. Physicians Insurers Association of America. Breast Cancer Study: 3rd Edition. Rockville, Md: 2002.

16. Physicians Insurers Association of America. Breast Cancer Study: 3rd Edition. Rockville, Md: 2002.

17. Physicians Insurers Association of America. Breast Cancer Study: 3rd Edition. Rockville, Md: 2002.

18. Physicians Insurers Association of America. Breast Cancer Study: 3rd Edition. Rockville, Md: 2002.

19. Physicians Insurers Association of America. Breast Cancer Study: 3rd Edition. Rockville, Md: 2002.

20. Physicians Insurers Association of America. Acute Myocardial Infarction Study. Rockville, Md: May 1996.

21. Physicians Insurers Association of America. Colon Cancer Study. Rockville, Md: 1991.

22. Physicians Insurers Association of America. Lung Cancer Study. Rockville, Md: 1992.

23. Physicians Insurers Association of America. Lung Cancer Study. Rockville, Md: 2004.

24. Physicians Insurers Association of America. Colon Cancer Study. Rockville, Md: 1991.

25. Physicians Insurers Association of America. . Lung Cancer Study. Rockville, Md: 1992.

26. Physicians Insurers Association of America. Lung Cancer Study. Rockville, Md: 2004.

27. Physicians Insurers Association of America. Colon Cancer Study. Rockville, Md: 1991.

28. Levinson W, Roter DL, et al. Physician—patient communication: the relationship with malpractice claims among primary care physicians and surgeons. *JAMA*. 1997; 277(7):553-559.

29. Physicians Insurers Association of America. Medication Error Study. Rockville, Md: 1993.

30. Physicians Insurers Association of America. Medical Errors Symposium White Paper, 2000.

31. Classen, D.C; et. al. "Adverse Drug Events in Hospitalized Patients." JAMA 1997: 277:301-6.

32. PIAA. Medical Errors Symposium White Paper, 2000.

33. Analysis of slip/fall related claims at the Harvard Medical Institutions. *Forum*. 1991; 12(1):2-5.

34. St Charles v. Kender, 38 Mass. App. Ct. 155 (1995)

35. Hand v Tavera and Humana Hospital, 864 SW 2d 678 (Tex. App. 1993)

36. Wickline v State of California., 228 Cal. Rptr. 661 (Cal. App. 2d. Dist. 1986)

37. Roop, Elizabeth S., "Pulling It Together — The HITECH Act & HIPAA" *For The Record* Vol. 21 No. 17 P. 10 (September 14, 2009).

38. Roop, Elizabeth S., "Pulling It Together — The HITECH Act & HIPAA" *For The Record* Vol. 21 No. 17 P. 10 (September 14, 2009).

39. Melamedia, LLC, *Annual Review of Medical Privacy and Security Enforcement.*

40. http://www.justice.gov/usao/are/news_release/ PDF_2009News_Releases/ July/3plea_ HIPAA_07202009.pdf

41. http://www.justice.gov/usao/are/news_releases/ PDFs_2009News_Releases/ July/3plea_ HIPAA_07202009.pdf

42. Kepler, Tara and McGinty, Charlene, "Telemedicine: How to Assess Your Risks and Develop a Program that Works," presentation at the American Health

Lawyers Association's Annual Hospitals and Health Systems Law Institute and Annual Physicians and Physician Organizations Institute, Phoenix, AZ (Feb. 10, 2009)

43. Kepler, Tara and McGinty, Charlene, "Telemedicine: How to Assess Your Risks and Develop a Program that Works," presentation at the *American Health Lawyers Association's Annual Hospitals and Health Systems Law Institute and Annual Physicians and Physician Organizations Institute,* Phoenix, AZ (Feb. 10, 2009)

44. Kepler, Tara and McGinty, Charlene, "Telemedicine: How to Assess Your Risks and Develop a Program that Works," presentation at the *American Health Lawyers Association's Annual Hospitals and Health Systems Law Institute and Annual Physicians and Physician Organizations Institute,* Phoenix, AZ (Feb. 10, 2009)

45. Kepler, Tara and McGinty, Charlene, "Telemedicine: How to Assess Your Risks and Develop a Program that Works," presentation at the *American Health Lawyers Association's Annual Hospitals and Health Systems Law Institute and Annual Physicians and Physician Organizations Institute,* Phoenix, AZ (Feb. 10, 2009)

46. Maheu, Dr. Marlene. *Telehealth: RISK MANAGEMENT IN THE RE-TOOLING OF HEALTH CARE;* Behavioral Information Tomorrow Conference; March 18-21, 1999, San Jose, California.

SCHEDULE FREE CONSULT

With experience helping thousands of doctors nationwide, we are confident that we can help you with your concerns or direct you to specialists who can.

If you would like to schedule a free consult, please complete this form and fax it to (817) 719-9144.

Please provide your email address, as we will be sending you a short form to complete before your consultation. This will help us more efficiently address your concerns while on the call.

Name: ____

Specialty: ____

Address: ____

____

City/State/Zip: _______________________________________

Phone: ____

Email: ____

Calls are done Monday through Friday between 8am and 7pm Eastern. Please provide your suggested times for your call.

1st choice: date: ___ / ___ time (eastern time): ___ : ___

2nd choice: date: ___ / ___ time (eastern time): ___ : ___

3rd choice: date: ___ / ___ time (eastern time): ___ : ___

4th choice: date: ___ / ___ time (eastern time): ___ : ___

Primary concerns: _____________________________________

____

____

FAX to (817) 719-9144

Discounted Books

The Physician's Money Manual teaches doctors the important lessons they never learned in medical school, residency or fellowship. Doctors learn how to efficiently leverage their time, money and effort so they can get more out of a medical practice. More specifically, doctors learn how to protect their personal and practice assets from lawsuits, taxes and bad investments while showing them the secrets to building wealth and avoiding catastrophic financial disasters. The Physician's Money Manual is a MUST HAVE for any physician wishing to achieve financial success.

Managing Risk: A Guide for Physicians and Practices is accredited for AMA PRA Credit. Co-written by a practicing physician, an attorney and a financial advisor, this monograph includes chapters on: providing care in today's malpractice environment, liability and the doctor-patient relationship, managing diagnosis-related liability, minimizing risks of miscommunication, managing high risk communication areas, managing the dangers of drug therapy, non-medical liability risks for the practicing physician, and liability in the new health care system.

Discounted Book Order Form

Book	Qty	Special Price	Total
The Physician's Money Manual (regularly $75)		$50	
Managing Risk: *A Guide for Physicians and Practices* (Approved for 7.5 *AMA PRA* *Category 1 Credits™*) (regularly $59.95)		$30	

Shipping & Handling $5 per item
Tax 8.25% in Texas
Tax 6.00% in Florida
Total

Credit Card: ___ ___ ___ ___ ___ ___ ___ ___ ___ ___ ___ ___ ___ ___ ___ ___

Exp Date: ___ ___ / ___ ___

Name: ______________________________

Phone: (______)_______-__________

Address: ______________________________

____

City/State/ZIP __________________________

Auth Signature: __________________________

FAX to (817) 719-9144

FREE ONLINE PDF

www.ingramcontent.com/pod-product-compliance
Lightning Source LLC
LaVergne TN
LVHW082350200926
848481LV00012B/3516